RELIGIOUS BODY:
Design for a New Reformation

RELIGIOUS BODY:

Design for a New Reformation

GABRIEL MORAN

A CROSSROAD BOOK

The Seabury Press · New York

The Seabury Press
815 Second Avenue
New York, N.Y. 10017

Copyright © 1974 by Gabriel Moran
Designed by Paula Wiener
Printed in the United States of America

LIBRARY OF CONGRESS CATALOGING IN PUBLICATION DATA

Moran, Gabriel.
  Religious body: design for a new reformation.

  "A Crossroad book."
  1. Church renewal. I. Title.
BV600.2.M65   262'.001   74–12103
ISBN 0–8164–1176–X

Contents

RELIGIOUS BODY:
Design for a New Reformation

Chapter One

Criteria
for Change

The title of this book, *Religious Body,* is an intentionally ambiguous term. It refers both to the physical organism (the body as religious) and to human organization (a body of religious people). Anthropologists have found that social organization and the image of the human body are interconnected in a particular society.[1] That is, organizations tend to have the same *kind* of unity as the human beings who construct them and live in them. For helpful insight on this relationship I am especially indebted to Norman O. Brown's *Love's Body*.[2] Although Brown did not apparently set out to write a book on religion, his examination of body (organism) as related to body (organization) quickly takes on a religious character. My intention is to investigate the religious phenomenon in relation to existing religious organizations.

The issue to be examined is the form that an organization needs to have to be appropriate for religious activity. There is, to begin with, a general problem of organization in the contemporary world. All organization is under some threat. Religious organization will have some of its own peculiar difficulties. What should also be noted is that unless the religious side of life is somehow faced, religion will almost certainly exacerbate the problem of human organization. Religion has an organizational problem and organization has a religious problem.

This thesis is difficult to accept for people whose attitude is either antireligious or nonreligious. They would prefer to dismiss the significance of religion. The mistake of recent centuries was to suppose that by politely disregarding religion or by dismissing it as childish it would slowly disappear. Even when liberal enlightenment and Marxist critique were joined by eulogies of Christian theology, religion did not go away. It is still very much with us and breaking out in new forms every day.

Whether the 1970s' reemergence of the religious phenomenon is regressive or whether it is a recovery of forgotten human values is the question before us. But I do not think that the issue can be posed without placing it into the context of religious organization. Many people who are writing and speaking on the religious upsurge deal with it in an individualistic setting that is outside the question of organization. In such an approach there is an implied denial that religion can be dealt with in a human way. Religious questions and religious activities are segregated into a private world; religion is allowed to exist as an idiosyncrasy. The result is that the enlightenment policy, touched up with a little more tolerance, is perpetuated. For the purpose of exempting their churches from ordinary human criticism, some ecclesiastical leaders readily accept the policy. However, the religious issue is being sidestepped in the tolerant allowance that a little religion will not do us any harm. One could suspect that the era bears some similarity to the Roman period of which Edward Gibbon said: "To the people all religions were equally true; to the philosophers equally false; and to the government equally useful."

While various new religions flourish outside the main-

stream of political, economic and social life, the old religions continue their old ways. Despite all of their
troubles, church and synagogue are still powerful systems
of organization. The reform of these organizations is more
and more left to the officials who have a vested interest
in seeing that business as usual continues. No basic reform
of the organization is to be expected from those who run
the current organization.

It may be objected that there are numerous reform
movements in Protestantism and an explosion of "renewal"
in Catholicism. One can readily admit that there are many
current reforms being attempted within these groups and
one can devoutly hope that some of the results will be
positive. However, a little skepticism might be in order.
It is not at all evident that there is any criterion for judging the reform. In the Catholic church it sometimes seems
that the *quantity* of change is the only thing at issue. Some
people seem to be against change, a posture which does
not fit anyone for reality anywhere. But such people may
be less naive and less dangerous than others who advocate
change, more change and every kind of change that fits
their plan for reality. Some people in the Catholic church
still confidently expect that with more time for the people
to accept the changes and with a few deaths in high places
the Catholic church will emerge shipshape and up-to-date.
One does not have to belong to that church's reactionary
wing to harbor doubts about the criteria being used for
church reform.

There is, of course, one criterion which is constantly
invoked. The Christian church is supposed to reform itself
according to the gospel. This supposed principle hides the
methodological problem of Christianity. Who decides what
gospel means? How can any organization be reformed on
the basis of ancient texts? Is not the very attempt to perpetuate ancient organizations by reforming them the rea-

son why religious organizations are inhibitive of human
life?

It is tempting to give an affirmative answer to the last
question and then proceed either to dismiss all "organized
religion" or to begin organizing a religion of one's own.
This double path has been the common approach in the
recent religious revival but I have claimed that this approach to religion is both inhuman and ineffective. There
might be another route: What is needed is a reform of
religious organization that is not intramurally ecclesiastical.

Reform of the Christian church has traditionally revolved around two poles: the new testament and the present situation (as perceived by some reformer). Every emphasis upon the present was seen to be a lessening of importance for the sacred writings. Every insistence upon
the writings seemed to be at the expense of relevancy
to the times. What I wish to present are some thoughts
about reform which are not based upon either of these two
poles, except insofar as these poles are included in a much
larger context of religious organization. On the one hand,
I contend that the new testament documents have no
answer for the question of religious organization today.
Presumably, some organizational practices would run
counter to much of what is in those documents but that
fact is not really of much practical help. On the other
hand, I contend that no religious organization ought to be
reconstructed to solve an outstanding problem of the day.
Religion is not a matter of being up-to-date or concerned
only with current fads. Presumably, some forms of religious organization would be so irrelevant as to be useless
but we have to go slowly on making a final judgment as
to what is religiously irrelevant.[3]

What I am trying to get at is that reforms within Christianity keep failing because the *method* of reform is part

of the problem needing reform. The content of reform packages has been far less important than who is doing the reforming and on what basis. Christianity has never been at a loss for high ideals and beautiful phrases. Reformers are always in favor of love, freedom, goodness, God, etc. But that kind of rhetoric can be compatible with religious organization that is sometimes innocuous, sometimes dangerous.

A criterion for the Christian church obviously has to go beyond the church. For the person judging, "to go beyond the church" does not mean spatially or temporally so much as psychologically and socially. The step is not easy because Christianity has traditionally frowned upon a person partaking of its life while retaining the personal autonomy to compare Christianity and other possible forms of religious life. Thus, the lack of criterion is no accident; the Christian church has considered the development of a criterion undesirable, if not blasphemous.

I have already mentioned the one way in which the Christian church has submitted to judgment, namely, the church is judged by the Christian scriptures. Reform movements based upon this principle are of an intramural kind and cannot go very far. An organization looking at some of its original literary output may be one element of reform but it is hardly the way to test an organization's viability and worth in relation to human life. Church officials could do worse than reading St. Matthew's gospel just as U.S. presidents could profit from reading the founding fathers of the United States. However, reading the new testament would be more analogous to reading the Declaration of Independence than to reading the Constitution.

Both liberal and conservative church officials are likely to reject the whole analogy. The Christian scriptures (and those it takes over from Judaism and calls its "old testament") are assumed to be without parallel. The claim is made that "standing under the scriptures" is submitting to the judgment of "God's Word." What a fundamentalist means by this statement is fairly clear. To be a consistent fundamentalist has become increasingly difficult, but if one is of fundamentalist mentality it is clear what kind of organization is entailed. It is much harder to pin down what liberal Christian people mean in referring to "God's Word." Any move in the direction of accepting the fact that the new testament writings were produced by Christian men in the first few centuries of the Christian era seems to evacuate any literal meaning to "God's Word." If some symbolic or metaphorical meaning is intended by the phrase, it can probably be sustained, but this change surely eliminates the one absolute around which Christian reforms have revolved. Adequate religious reform cannot be based upon the residue of fundamentalist thinking.

2

The subtitle of this work, "design for a new reformation," points to this methodological problem left unresolved by the Protestant reformation. That the problem could not be seen, let alone solved, in the sixteenth century is understandable enough but that Catholics and Protestants of the twentieth century continue the same procedure is truly amazing. In fact, one of the clearest directions of Roman Catholicism in the last ten to fifteen years has been to adopt as its own the Protestant principle of criticizing the church on the basis of scripture. Taken by itself, that principle has proved to be inadequate. That the Roman church had much to learn from Protestant churches only the most narrow-minded reactionaries denied but that Christianity would be improved by the Catholic church becoming Protestant is extremely doubtful.

In the late medieval world the burning religious question was where to find the true and authentic church of Jesus Christ in the midst of a corrupt church. The criteria of a reformed and purified church are found in John Calvin's words: "Wherever we see the Word of God purely preached and heard, and the sacraments administered according to Christ's institution, there, it is not to be doubted, a church of God exists." [4] Today it would not be helpful to put the question as a search for a church. That word is so totally controlled by the current institution that it cannot provide a starting point of discussion. I have no intention of relinquishing the word church but I also choose not to begin with church as the basic category to rethink organization. There is no way in which the word church can provide sufficient maneuverability for the questions I wish to raise.[5]

The thesis of this book may now be stated in briefest form: The earlier reformation period held that the true church exists where the word is preached and the sacraments are administered. In today's reformation period we may judge that a valid religious body arises where education and community join to reveal the religious expressions of human life. In each case we have two criteria, or a twofold criterion. The several differences in principle between the reformations can be immediately noted: (1) We move from speaking of *the* one true *church* to *a* valid religious *body*. (2) We move from the preaching of words to education. (3) We move from the distributing of sacraments to communities. (4) We look now for the presence of religious expression wherever community and education interpenetrate. I shall argue that as education and community fully converge, community and religious community become synonymous as do education and religious education.

In the case of both preaching and sacraments the Christian church was on the right track, but the criteria are inadequate today and need reformulation. The danger in the expanded version offered above is that the new criteria may seem to be too general. Religious bodies do need specificity and concreteness. The following chapters of this book will try to show that these new criteria are not vague generalities. My descriptions, it is true, will not exclude all debate and ambiguity, but education and community nonetheless do provide a firm and logical basis for talking about religious bodies. Christian people have plenty of particular details which might fill out the framework. What is desperately needed is a point at which to begin conversation across all religious lines, namely, between individuals and institutions, between different religious groups, between the religious and nonreligious sides of an individual's life.

The argument to be developed in chapter five is that education has to replace preaching if the existing Christian church is to be a religious body. In the sixteenth century, preaching was conceived to be a worthwhile activity. In the twentieth century there is probably no place except the Christian church where the verb "to preach" is supposed to have a positive meaning. The continuance of this strange anachronism is not an accident. Preaching is at the center of Christianity; not so much what the minister does at 11:00 A.M. Sundays but what the ecclesiastical institution does all the time. In Roman Catholic writing the words preach and teach are used interchangeably; the practice is so common one hardly notices it. Most Catholics may never reflect on the fact that preaching and teaching are different to the point of being opposites.

There is, of course, endless criticism of church sermons but the criticism misses the point. One does not try to improve what should not exist in the first place. In fact, the improvement of what is negative in value could itself be negative. Hardly anyone is misled by the droning of pious clichés that is found around the radio dial on Sunday morning. Some relevancy, wit or candor would simply hide the fact that there is an insoluble problem of form with sermons.

The sermon from the pulpit is both a central activity of the Christian church and a symptom of what the church is. One does not tamper lightly with an organization's central and epitomizing activity. Preaching is central to the life of the Protestant minister and ironically it has become only recently more central to the priest's work. To think of eliminating preaching is of course to consider eliminating preachers. Criticizing bad sermons has always been fair game even for clergymen, but challenging the fact of preaching is a quite different matter. Although I have no desire to attack anyone's life or profession, the question of preaching cannot be avoided.

The defense of the activity of preaching is based upon something deeper than just professional security. Preaching is traced back to Jesus and Paul so that "proclaiming the gospel" or "preaching the word" is taken to be what Christianity *is*. One could begin by pointing out that the church's translation of these phrases from the first to the twentieth centuries is a wooden one. However, the problem cannot be resolved that easily. Christianity from the start has been a religion which told everyone else what the truth is. Christianity has also been other than that and more than that but the wordy and preachy aspects may indeed be inseparable from what Christianity is. This fact raises the question of whether Christianity can be a valid religious body. The question is hardly a new one; generations of Jews or Hindus have raised it before. What may be new is the possibility of raising the issue *within* the Christian tradition and of asking what it implies for church reorganization.

Up to now, it has been assumed that the church requires preaching; therefore, preaching is good. Suppose that one begins from the other end: Preaching is bad; Christianity requires preaching; therefore, Christianity requires a different kind of reformation than has occurred in the past and to the extent that the result may not be Christianity. Certainly, it has to be considered whether the abstract noun Christianity should not be put to rest as soon as possible. There is more chance of saving the term Christian church, but only if assumptions deeply embedded in Christian language are unearthed and challenged. My main point for the moment is that the Christian religion cut off from its Jewish roots and out of relation to the other primitive and developed religions of the world is a dangerous religion and the danger is evident in the fact that it preaches.

3

The other great concern of the earlier reformation period was that the sacraments were to be validly distributed. Here also the Christian church had an instinct for the right question but the manner of dealing with it has been inadequate. Instead of a sacramental principle invigorating church life, the discussion of sacraments has taken place in narrow ecclesiastical confinement. A rationalistic and verbose church tends to reduce sacraments to sermons.

The sixteenth century was concerned about such things

as the number of sacraments, whether and how Christ instituted each sacrament, the necessary matter and form,
the validity of orders, etc. Questions of this kind could
still have significance in intramural church discussions
but they easily distract from the crucial question of
whether the Christian church is a religious body at all. Is
there anything that can realistically be called a religious
community, that is, a group of people who are united in
a set of religious practices?

Almost in spite of itself the Christian church functioned
as a religious body through its sacramental life. Not that
its sacraments ever functioned very well but even in a
weakened state the sacramental activity enabled the body
to survive. There was from the start a problem with sacraments, and very early a wall was erected between those
who gave out sacraments and those who received them.
The sixteenth century saw an attempt to break through
that wall but the times were not ripe for understanding
sacraments. Whatever Protestantism might have accomplished and whatever success it has had, there is one thing
that the main Protestant tradition has clearly not done,
namely, eliminate the division between clergy and laity,
a phrase which for clarity's sake should be translated eliminate the clergy.

Within Roman Catholicism, a sacramental life continued to hold people together. The typical Catholic paid
lip service to there being seven sacraments, but in practice each group had its seventeen or seventy sacramental
activities: devotions to St. Francis or St. Philomena, bene-
diction and visits to the blessed sacrament, triduums and
novenas, rosaries and infants of Prague. Much of this activity may have been unhealthy; certainly it was illogical.
But one should also carefully note that the activity did
exist and it was the religious expression of functioning
groups.

These activities may seem as strange as the totemistic cults of a primitive Australian clan. But just as we have come to be more tolerant and understanding of aborigines we may be in need of tolerance closer to home. One thing that has been learned about so-called primitive tribes is that you do not obliterate their strange religious activities and expect them to shape up into upstanding middle-class citizens of the so-called advanced world. This point was unfortunately overlooked in recent Catholic reforms. That Catholic devotional life needed pruning or reform is hardly denied by anyone. But who were the reformers free enough of self-delusion to bring about the change?

There had emerged in Europe at the turn of this century a triple movement: ecumenical, catechetical and liturgical. The coalition of these three was both the strength and the weakness of the movement. If ecumenical had been defined as something broader than intra-Christian, perhaps the other two components would have had more chance of success. There was both narrowness and irony in the Catholic church staking its hope for liturgical revival by turning to Protestanism.

Liturgy became the key reform word in Catholic life; the word had all kinds of subversive overtones. The liturgy, it was said, is not the distributing of sacraments but the activity of the people. If the Roman church were indeed to become the community of Catholic people that would be a revolution without parallel. But as always in such movements, the result being sought was not so clear as it was assumed to be. There was also the inevitable conflict implicit in giving something back to "the people" while a large segment of the people were not seeking for that.

A liturgical movement crystallized in the United States in the 1940s, remaining the concern of a small and esoteric group until the late 1950s. Then as part of a liberal movement in the Catholic church the liturgical movement exploded with great splash and unrealistic expectations. At the same time as this explosion, the official church embraced and engulfed the movement. The Second Vatican Council not only accepted the movement but outdid the reformers in exaggerated claims for what was now officially defined as liturgy. Most of the reformers thought that they had won the war because they had trained their sights on several particular reforms judged to be symptomatic of a new church. Many Episcopalians stood by amused and astounded at the euphoria caused by the introduction of English into the Roman liturgy. Episcopalians were heard to whisper that the vernacular was not a panacea for the church's problems.

As should have been expected, reforms like the vernacular proved to be a mixed blessing. What succeeded the Latin mystery of nonverbal sharing was Latin translations which people were to participate in by following the priest's instructions. There was a rise in rational comprehension, but the inherent problem of the church being preachy and verbose was also heightened. Many of "the people" complained because the activities which had stabilized their lives were eliminated as unliturgical. The old woman who wanted to "tell her beads" during mass was dismissed as a benighted reactionary but it may be that she was in touch with a wider catholic and religious tradition than those who measured everything by their reading of a first century book.

The question of change in the church was too easily cast into the framework of liberal versus conservative. Actually, there seems to be a different understanding of symbols, community and religion, and the self-deception is not all on one side. An anthropologist studying the resistance of British Catholics to the elimination of Friday abstinence comments:

To take away one symbol that meant something is no guarantee that the spirit of charity will flow in its place. It might have been safer to build upon that small symbolic wall in the hope that eventually it could come to surround Mount Sion. But we have seen that those who are responsible for ecclesiastical decisions are only too likely to have been made, by the manner of their education, insensitive to non-verbal signals and dull to their meaning. This is central to the difficulties of Christianity today. It is as if the liturgical signal boxes were manned by colour-blind signalmen.[6]

The liturgical movement thus ended by reenforcing the clericalist, anticommunal prayer that it set out to criticize. Saying that the liturgical movement ended may seem premature but it certainly appears that the movement which began in 1900 found its completion in 1965. One may hope that there is some parallel here with the feminist movement which once concentrated its energies on suffrage and seemed to have exhausted itself with winning that one small gain. As a reinvigorated feminist movement has begun which will not settle for small gestures, one can hope that the Catholic church has a liturgical movement in its future which will return prayer to the people. What the liturgical reformers could not see was that you return prayer to the people not by translating the canon or standing for communion but by eliminating those who took over the prayer life of the people, namely, the clergy. It is not surprising that the liturgical reformers could not see this point since most of them were priests.

As things now stand the discussion of sacraments and liturgy has returned to being an in-house topic, almost totally the preserve of priests and official documents. At a time when sacramental symbolism is reemerging as a universal issue the Catholic church is caught in preposterously narrow arguments which no one can win. An example is the 1973 decree from Rome that the experiment was over that allowed children to go to confession after first communion. The pronouncement drew expected cries of outrage from catechists and threats of disobedience from rebellious priests. The energy seems expended in a useless battle which could possibly disintegrate current authority patterns but more likely will strengthen the whole system.

It is difficult to find anyone asking what would seem to be the more obvious questions: Why should children go to confession at all? Why should adults go to confession? Isn't it a fact that few adults do go anymore? Is there anything of validity in this peculiar rite and if so what kind of form would it have to take today? What do all those people talking on both sides of the subject do in their own lives? While the church fiddles from Rome over administering confession to six-year-olds, and opponents fight the prescription but accept the legitimacy of such prescriptions, the sacrament of penance is almost totally inoperative and the entire sacramental structure is not far behind.

The solution does not lie in bishops discussing the right topics at national conventions. Nor will better letters from the chancery office help. Chancery letters are part of the problem, not part of the answer. If there is an answer it consists of years or generations of effort to establish working religious communities that could rediscover some of the Christian activities. In the present example: A person may rediscover a rite of confessing one's faults to one's sisters and brothers because that is just what a religious body has to do to exist, as some people have already rediscovered in their own experience.

4

The reference above to chancery letters raises a further
question about the methodology of this book. To write a
book on how to reform the church is to get caught in the
very problem that needs reform. That is, nearly all books
in the Christian church follow the literary genre of chancery communiqué. The standard elements are: (1) something is wrong with the world; (2) tell people what the
truth is and expect them to correct the world; (3) when
things do not improve, say it again louder. Conservative
and liberal reforms tend to employ this same method.
Christianity did not invent the preacher of reform but it
flooded the market with practitioners.

So much is chancery communiqué the only accepted
category of writing in the Christian church that all books
on religion and morality are judged on that standard. If
one writes a book describing what is evil, one is liable to
be condemned for advocating what is evil. That a book's
method could be a description of fact rather than advice on
curing problems does not find easy acceptance in church
circles.

The problem is the traditional one of conflict between
artist and society. The artist is often judged harshly not
for the artistic results but for the method of exposing
reality and for failing to fix up the world to make it look
better.

As a pertinent example, especially in reference to the
church, I would like to refer to the book and movie entitled *Clockwork Orange*. The work portrays extraordinary
violence and destructive clashes. The movie was condemned in many places because of its violence though in
many other places it was thought to have redeeming value

because it at least defended free will. After all of the controversy over the film, the novelist Anthony Burgess has made this interesting comment:

> What had the film done? It has allegedly encouraged violence, which, so far as I can see, needs no encouragement. . . . Everything seems to miss the argument the author himself has against his own book (and by extension the film made out of it)—that it was didactic rather than pornographic, since it preached the necessity of free choice, and that it is not the job of a work of art to be didactic. As they say, if you want to send a message, go to Western Union.[7]

Although I cannot make great artistic claims for the present book, I do wish it to be judged on aesthetic principles, that is, on whether the pieces fit together into appropriate form. I am not interested in writing a book to reform the Christian church but I am interested in describing a religious world which includes the Christian church. The issue that quickly surfaces is whether one has a language that is adequate to the job. Thus, there are two inseparable components of this method: the description of things as they are and the development of a language adequate to do so. The procedure is almost the reverse of most church writing, which assumes that the words are available and advocates that the world should be different. My wish is to start with the world as it is and advocate that language should be different.

The first part of this method, trying to describe what appears, is, I have claimed, basic to art. The same approach operates in the physical sciences. Alfred North Whitehead describes the work of science as an intense looking at what is before us. Explanations end in ultimate arbitrariness, but good explanations disclose general principles of reality that stretch beyond our explicit powers of discernment. In

short, Whitehead writes: "The sheer statement of what
things are may contain elements explanatory of why things
are." [8]

The temptation is to jump over the things that exist
to explain why they are this way and how they could be
better. Religions have functioned ambiguously on this
question, sometimes reconciling people to their situation
by providing a ritual, sometimes pointing their minds to
some other better world. Western Christianity has been
particularly attracted to producing plans for making the
world better. Although there is a good element to this
drive, it can produce an impatient heavy-handedness with
those who do not agree and a peculiar self-delusion on
the part of church leaders.

The Second Vatican Council is a striking illustration
of this point. Vatican II has been widely hailed for being
a positive council. It did not merely condemn things but
set forward a package of reform. In presuming to produce
such a platform, however, ecclesiastical leaders were reenforcing some of the worst aspects of their authoritarian
structure. The fact of the Council was undoubtedly positive and the reverberations will continue for decades. The
meeting might have been of more value if the participants
had burned their documents on the last day. The suggestion is not made flippantly. The bishops had said what
they were capable of saying to each other. The sixteen
documents were outdated by the last day of the Council.
Alas, the bishops went home with the documents, study
groups were organized and quoting the Council became a
favorite liberal pastime. As each year goes by, however, the
documents get more and more quoted on the right. The
shift is not surprising. Documents of reform issued from
an authoritarian body cannot be "liberal" no matter what
the documents say.

The description of Vatican II as authoritarian may seem

unfair. The adjective does not mean that each individual
was an authoritarian personality but that the principles
on which the body was organized were extremely narrow.
The way in which the Catholic church generates its officials
has been guaranteed to produce an authoritarian attitude
in its meetings and decisions. If Vatican II had wished to
do something positive, it might have concentrated on doing what it could to make Vatican III a more truly ecumenical council. Granted that this change would be no
easy task, it might have made Vatican II a little more reti-
cent in preaching to the human race.

My main concern here is the fatal flaw in the Christian
understanding of communication and change. Catholic
officials still express confidence that the documents of Vatican II at least tell us how the church and the world should
look; the only remaining problem is to apply the knowledge. There is a failure to recognize that reform platforms
from unreformed bodies are themselves obstacles to seeing
what is there. Individuals or groups who tell the rest of the
world to change are naive in thinking their advice will be
followed and presumptuous in thinking they have the right
to give such advice. Catholic officials might profit from a
reading of the Hasidic master Baal Shem. In a story called
"The Limits of Advice," the rabbi is asked by a disciple
how to know whether a celebrated figure is a true master.
Baal Shem answers: "Ask him to advise you what to do to
keep unholy thoughts from disturbing you in your prayers
and studies. If he gives you advice, then you will know
that he belongs to those who are of no account." [9]

5

The other part of my methodological concern, the ade-
quacy of language, is implicit in the example of Vatican

II. Communication does not occur by thoughts being placed into available words which are stored on paper. Communication presupposes a shared life which words can illuminate. I will comment in chapter six on the political use of speech. Here I wish to concentrate on the tension between precision and ambiguity as well as between particularity and universality in the use of speech.

Language is the humans' oldest and most precious possession. It differentiates the humans from the other animals and it is the specifically human way to interact with the world. Speech is the human alternative to violence in changing the world. Like other precious human gifts speech is common, ordinary and unassuming, and it is thereby vulnerable to continual abuse and mishandling. Politicians, poets, writers and schoolteachers have an obligation to preserve the vitality of language. Religion should be especially sensitive to the depths, nuances and magical overtones of words. In a well-known definition, Wittgenstein described philosophy as "a battle against the bewitchment of our intelligence by means of language." [10] The definition acknowledges that language is of its nature "bewitching." Language always needs criticizing but the elimination of bewitchment would not be desirable even if it were possible.

A precise use of language, therefore, does not exclude all ambiguity. To use language precisely is to have a feeling for its roots and all its flavors in living exchange. A poet working with language plays upon all the levels of feeling sedimented in ordinary speech. One cannot rid the world of simple old words just because they are ambiguous. As Martin Buber insisted, one must fight for the old words, recreating them daily in a living community.[11] One temptation for circumventing the difficulties of language is to manufacture words which supposedly will not be am-

biguous. Worse still is the blurring of meaning in a care-
less phrasing with the added comment that the words are
not important because we know what is meant.

The rich, living words of a language need a precise
and actual focus, but this demand does not exclude a
universal quality. One reaches the universal through and in
the particular so that one test of the actuality of genuine
reference is whether the word is also open to being filled
in by the human race. If any group uses a word which
belongs to everyone as if it were their sole possession, they
destroy the value of the word even for their own purposes.
Conversely, when words are invented by a group and the
words convey nothing to the rest of the race, one must
suspect that the words do not convey any human meaning
within the group.

I shall try to demonstrate in the next chapter the importance of an institution's control of language, and the
possibility of discovering new answers when the words are
available to ask the right questions. My concern here is
the caring for one's language and being conscious of what
is contained in apparent accidents of speech. Nothing is
more disconcerting than to have someone say: "Isn't that
only a semantic problem?" What could be more important
in any discussion than a semantic problem? If we have
gotten so far as a recognition of semantics we are at the
heart of the matter. C. Wright Mills, after a devastating
critique of some opaque writing in the field of sociology,
summed up the problems of ambitious theorizing:

> Grand theory is drunk on syntax, blind to semantics.
> Its practitioners do not truly understand that when
> we define a word we are merely inviting others to
> use it as we would like it to be used, that the purpose
> of definition is to focus argument upon fact, and that

the proper result of good definition is to transform
arguments over terms into disagreements about fact,
and thus open arguments to further inquiry.[12]

Mills indicates here why the advocacy of linguistic
change is the proper role for religious writing, especially
with reference to Christianity. The danger of writing on
Christianity is that one is liable to preach reform while
the preaching of reform is itself the problem. But advocacy of linguistic change cannot be preached, it can only
be demonstrated in dialogue. Manipulation is reduced to
a minimum because there is brought to consciousness what
the words do. The other person always has space to get
out of the way and in fact must suspend judgment to see
the working out of a full pattern. What is incumbent on
those who advocate linguistic change is that they offer a
speech pattern which saves all that the other holds dear
while opening up new possibilities.

This policy of restricted advocacy may seem to be a
ridiculously insufficient way to cope with life's problems.
Linguistic change is not the only kind of change needed
in the world but it is probably the place to begin. In any
case, it is what a writer must usually be content with to accomplish anything as writer. My advocacy is for precision
and comprehensiveness of language. What follows upon
a change of speech is not particularly for writers to decide.

In this concern with method and language in religious
writing I would disagree with the principles expressed at
the beginning of Harvey Cox's *The Seduction of the
Spirit*.[13] Cox divides the uses of language into story and
signal. He claims that there should be a balance between
the two and that religion must today emphasize the story
to regain a balance with signals. On this basis Cox's book
is largely a recounting of personal testimony and a description of "people's religion."

This method hardly touches upon the profound problem in the area of religious writing; taken alone the method could be quite misleading. First, while it is an important function of religion to preserve stories it does not follow that religious writing has the function of telling stories. There is room for journalistic accounts and the recounting of stories but we have plenty of that already. What is more obviously lacking is a critical kind of writing that would test out these stories in relation to life and thought. Second, to say that we have an excess of signal over story is true only in the most superficial sense. We may have an excess quantity of signals but we do not have the coherent, integral and intelligible framework of thought desperately needed today. Third, balance is the wrong word here. It is the *division* into story and signal that is destructive. The only way to overcome the schizophrenia of our lives is to integrate the two so that stories are humanized further because related to critical thinking.

Unfortunately, "testimony" is a perpetuation of the standard Christian method which fails to be dialogical because it does not submit its own language to critique. For that reason, testimony has traditionally been a coercive mode whether or not the speaker intends coercion. The standard Christian testimony has come from the bible. If one must have testimony the new testament is better than most substitutes. There is doubtful progress in going to autobiographical testimony or the testimony of "people's religion." An acute problem is the significance of one person's testimony and the selective principle for the "people's religion." Are we not at the end of such testimony left with more data that can only function as signals in other people's lives? The Christian church is in a cul-de-sac of its own linguistic making and it would seem that the role of writers on the subject is to suggest some ways of speaking that would open a door.

6

As example, and more than example, of what I mean, I am using the word Christian in this book only as an adjective to describe an existing group. This kind of insistence may seem to some readers innocuous, to other readers arbitrary and to others offensive. My only defense is that if we try that usage it would enable us to know better what we are talking about and make it easier to talk with more people. We would be saved from reference to what a Christian is or how a Christian acts when in fact there is no agreed-upon meaning of the noun. Logically we could use Christian as a noun to refer to membership in the Christian organization but the noun has become so overlaid with individualistic and ideal essences that it is better to avoid the nominal use altogether.

It should have been clear at least by the end of the nineteenth century that there is no essence to Christianity. Talk about how "the Christian" acts floats vaguely about a world of ideal images. In contrast, if one says Christian church, Christian movement, Christian religion, etc., one describes something historically and socially real. With the adjective there remain shades at the edges and plenty of room for debate on what constitutes the mainstream and what are rivulets. That kind of discussion could be fruitful and it also gives us space to move around in. One can consider trying to heighten some aspects and play down other emphases in what has been and is a socially diverse movement. Christian as an adjective is not a compliment or a virtue, it is a designation of a group of people who have done some good things and some bad things in their time.

The use of the word Christian as an adjective would

lessen the rampant antiinstitutionalism within the Christian church as well as the hidden imperialism that accompanies protest in the name of "being a Christian." The attitude is reflected in the title and contents of John Robinson's *The Difference in Being a Christian Today*.[14] Although he proclaims the end of "stable state" Christianity, he has no doubt about the noun Christian expressing some kind of ideal essence. Robinson quotes approvingly the statement of Fred Brown: "There are more Christians outside than inside the church." [15] At first sight this kind of statement looks merely foolish or masochistic but there is a hidden arrogance to it. The noun Christian is being pushed on all kinds of people who want no part of it. The ideal for which everyone is supposed to strive is to be a Christian, a word which church officials can appropriate to themselves whenever it is convenient. At the same time such officials can avoid the responsibility of doing something about improving the organization for which everyone else in the world uses the word Christian. Such is the menace of anticlerical clergymen.

The Christian church will probably not improve: (1) by people leaving it; (2) by people attacking it; (3) by admonitions that it ought to be made up of better people. There is a chance of change for the better if people can continue to use many of their key words but in a way that opens dialogue across barriers. Most of the world knows only too well what the term Christian church(es) refers to. Dialogue on that subject is possible and the dialogue could be fruitful. But as soon as boundaries are denied to this human organization and it begins spreading "anonymously" or "latently" throughout the world, the old suspicions return. Here is a group that wants to claim as theirs anything in the whole world that is good while denying responsibility for what is bad even though it is patently within their tradition or organization. An adjectival use of Christian does not exclude this tendency but the focus can be more easily kept if we are talking of something open to public view, something that surely exists and is describable.

The question at this point may be: Why bother? Why go through a painfully long process of trying to change an institution when its ways are so set? The answer implied at the beginning of this chapter is that there is no alternative. If there is need for realistic speech within the Christian church, there is also need for realism on the part of those who are not church members. Jewish and Christian religions have existed for millennia; they still exist today. Each child born in the Western world ineluctably acquires a powerful relationship to these religions. One does not get rid of the influence of a Christian church by simply deciding not to belong. Nor can one reconstitute a religious life for oneself by disregarding existing religious institutions. If one tries to go that route, bits and pieces of the Christian past are liable to function mindlessly in the new religion or one gets caught in constructing a counter-church.

Much of the new religion seems bizarre and utterly without roots in this hemisphere but that is the way a counter-church looks. At any religious gathering in this country one can meet individuals who say: "I left the church. I am much more radical than that. I'm into this special form of Eastern meditation and I have this totally unified vision of the world." Subsequent conversation, however, often reveals someone bitterly at odds with the Christian church but attacking the church with the church's own imperialistic language. It is not easy to get free of that language and its consequences either in the life of an individual or the foreign policy of a country.

This problem is reflected in Theodore Roszak's *Where the Wasteland Ends.*[16] Roszak is a leading spokesman of

those in search of a new religion and his book contains
fascinating and valuable material. He makes it clear that
he was brought up within the Christian church but now
wants no part of a church. Much of the negative part of
his critique is a powerful indictment of the church but
the positive program that emerges is less satisfying. It may
be said that this is always the case and that the critic's job
is not to supply an alternative system. I could agree to that
point and in fact have insisted that critics of the Christian
church should resolutely avoid a reform package.

What I have claimed as necessary in any religious
criticism is: (1) that we find a realistic point of entry to
people's lives; (2) that we speak in a way which allows
us to affirm our lives while also freeing us from intolerance. Roszak produces an amalgam of religious elements
whose relation to existing people is not clear. He is in
danger of doing what he (rightly) considers the fault of
the churches, namely, that they impose an ideology upon
people's experience. Roszak puts great stock in what he
calls the "old gnosis," the visionary light of Eastern and
mystery religions which preceded Christianity.[17] But even
if the "old gnosis" is desirable, the fact is that the Christian and Jewish traditions exist and have worked irre-
versible change in the world that preceded them. There
is no way out of our religious predicament except by going
forward from what exists today, and what exists is a world
affected for better or worse by the rise of Jewish and
Christian traditions in the West.

This concern with what exists now in no way belittles
study of the past. The only way to make sense of where
we are is to trace the origins of our religious situation.
Roszak has some valuable things to say about "sacramental
symbolism" but there is more that can be done with this
category if it is connected to medieval Catholicism. Certainly, one can use a broader meaning than the Catholic

church has used but the inclusion of Catholic tradition in the discussion is both more realistic and more effective. I am not suggesting that anyone like Roszak should be writing on Roman decrees on confession. But a really "radical" approach to sacramental symbolism would have to examine the existing churches and their past.

There is no going backward in time but there is possible a recovery of what we thought we had left behind. It is not so much going back as going down and going in and going beyond. The past is sedimented in our bones, flesh, blood, dreams and psyche, but most of all in our language. "Anthropology is history, and history is etymology." [18] Changing some key words in one's language is as difficult as correcting a stutter. One does not do it by willing it or thinking about it but by recovering one's childhood and going down into one's intestines. At the end of all our attempts we will still stutter because "civilization originates in stammering . . . the builder is a stutterer . . . the thunder is God stuttering." [19] But the stutter will now be the human problem of trying to capture in words what cannot ultimately be put there rather than the stutter being false controls which we have imposed on ourselves.

7

My search here is for criteria by which to judge a new reformation. The criteria are found in a language that bridges human differences because it is rooted deeply in human history and imagery. My use of the term "new reformation" is a reference to Paul Goodman's *New Reformation: Notes of a Neolithic Conservative*.[20] Goodman's complaint is that the contemporary form of conservatism does not try to conserve much. Conservatives seem to want to turn the clock back to the age of McKinley. What we need, he claims, is a "neolithic" conservatism that would rediscover and love the past that is part of our present.[21]

Goodman's point is particularly apt in reference to religion. Those who are called conservative in the Christian church seem intent on preserving the sixteenth century or texts from the first century. A religious conservative should presumably be interested in the originating forces which gave birth to the Christian movement as well as other religions. That kind of conservatism would probably conflict with the contemporary church institution, which veers dangerously from an unhistorical orthodoxy called conservatism to a faddish relevancy called liberalism. The split is so severe that it is nearly impossible to write on the Christian church without being immediately dismissed by one side or the other. The attempt here is to find a different ground with a purified language which would not be easily classifiable as conservative or liberal. In the new reformation already well advanced the questions transcend the intramural fights between liberal and conservative church people. What we have to respond to is the religious and social world that confronts us.

Chapter Two

Domesticating
Human Power

The thesis set forward in chapter one was that the validity of a religious body can be judged by whether it arises from the intersection of community and education. A description of such a body (chapter six) requires a separate consideration of these three concepts: religion (chapter three), community (chapter four) and education (chapter five). Before treating each of these concepts individually, it will be helpful in this chapter to see the relationship in which these three terms currently stand. I am interested in the most general pattern of community, education and religion but I will focus on the development that has taken place in the United States.

As I have explained in chapter one, a description of community, education and religion is mainly a description of how the words have been used. It is useless to speculate on the great possibilities of community, education or religion unless one first grasps how the words are now used and why they are used that way. Whoever owns the words owns the world. If the words are not available to ask the right questions, then no new answers are possible. Society as a whole and institutions within society prevent certain kinds of change by not allowing for the language that would be necessary to raise questions of that kind of change. If a person tries to ask a question for which no language is available, that person is likely to be judged either silly or crazy.

The Western world has been dominated in recent centuries by a pattern of life that can be almost entirely summarized in one word: bureaucracy. The word bureaucracy is not introduced here as a shibboleth or a slogan with which to attack every organization. Bureaucracy is one form of organization, and this distinction is crucial if we are to have other forms of organization. Bureaucracy is largely the invention of the modern West though it had its beginnings in the ancient world and has now spread throughout the whole modern world.

There is considerable agreement in the social sciences on the distinguishing characteristics of bureaucracy. There is also general agreement on the fact that bureaucracy has been a short-term success in running a technological world. There is less consensus on other questions: (1) Is bureaucracy neutral or does it carry within itself its own ethos and ethic? (2) Is it possible or likely that bureaucracy may self-destruct if and when it is carried beyond its limits? (3) Largely a combination of the two preceding questions: What limitations does bureaucracy need to have to be a positive factor in human life rather than a destructive one? My concern in this chapter is with the cloudy area that these three questions touch upon.

There are a variety of ways to describe bureaucracy but the main outlines of it are clear. Carl Friedrich has listed six elements in the bureaucratic pattern. Those elements are: (1) concentration of control and supervision; (2) differentiation of function; (3) qualification for office; (4) objectivity; (5) precision and consistency; (6) discretion.[1] Each of these characteristics can be described in positive terms or else in words with pejorative overtone. For example, concerning the flow of information, one can accurately speak either of a restriction of data to make information operate more effectively or of secrecy that keeps each individual from knowing what is going on. Perhaps as a general rule, those at the top of the organization use the positive phrases (at least in public) and those at the bottom use the negative descriptions.

The difference in phrasing is of no little importance. But in either case, the main thing to be noted about the characteristics is that bureaucracy is simply the metaphor of the machine imposed on human relationships. A peculiar self-mirroring process was at work here: bureaucracy began as an imitation of the machine in order to produce machines; as more machines were produced, the organization became more machinelike. The reciprocal perfection of image and counter image can go on almost, but not quite, indefinitely. One need not propound conspiratorial views of history or complicated economic theories to grasp the inherent problem of bureaucracy: for its own perfection bureaucracy moves relentlessly in the direction of eliminating human elements while at the same time it is the human beings who must control and direct bureaucracy.

The problem is an enormous one and there is no obvious ready-made solution for it. Certainly, it does little good and perhaps does harm to pretend that individualistic pieties are the answer to what is an incredibly complicated problem of systems. One way of answering the problem is to say that political life must control economic life rather than vice versa. While this principle is correct its easy assumption could obscure the terrible bind we are in, namely, that political organization, having become as bureaucratic as business corporations, can hardly play the part of controller. The slogans of political parties cannot get at the problem of the *form* which political life has taken. The issue that Michael Harrington's *Socialism* constantly returns to is: Where the state owns the means of production the question is who owns the state? [2] Whatever the supposed form of government, in the absence of effective political participation, the only possible owner of the state is the elite of a bureaucratic class structure.

In choosing to analyze community, education and religion I am trying to get behind this political question. Politics needs help from other sources of human power and other forms of human relationship. Politics will inevitably be corrupted by business unless there is a social life, a religious life and a life of learning and leisure. The key to a political life having adequate political form is its relation to these other forms of life. However, as we shall see and as one could guess, community, education and religion have themselves not escaped engulfment by the dominant organizational form.

If we first restrict consideration to the business and economic world, bureaucracy seems to have its most appropriate and successful sphere of operation. The modern West has been extraordinarily productive of goods and services. Technology and bureaucracy have worked as hand and glove in the flow of material goods. The modern business world is almost unthinkable without the orderliness, precision, punctuality, division of labor and chain of command which are the hallmarks of bureaucracy.

All is not well, however, even within the home territory. While profits were still running high there developed strange rumblings within the business world and some hand wringing on the part of business executives. For the last twenty-five years many companies have tried with varying success to adapt to new needs. There is, for example, the nagging problem of worker motivation and satisfaction that cannot be cured by salary increases. That kind of problem may be symptomatic of deep-seated problems in the system as a whole. The complexity of the ecological relationships today and the problems of worldwide production and distribution might be beyond anyone's understanding and control. It is not obvious that bureaucracy must have an upper limit of size, but that may be the case. It is also not clear whether national conglomerates and multi-national corporations are evidence to the contrary or examples of a relentless logic that risks destruction for the sake of expansion.

The only point I wish to make for the moment is that even in the business world bureaucracy may have its limits. Certainly, there are particular times when bureaucracy gets in its own way. As Robert Merton phrased it: Elements that are conducive to efficiency in general lead to inefficiency in specific instances.[3] In times of crisis, bureaucracy, by reason of its own virtues, cannot easily and quickly right itself. That fact is beyond doubt. The question now generalized from this fact is whether we have reached a stage in history where the crisis is a whole era. In this case, bureaucracy would have been so successful in its production that it has produced the means for its own elimination. It is this situation which Warren Bennis and Philip Slater discuss under the heading of a postbureaucratic world.[4] They argue that when change becomes rapid and diverse in kind bureaucracy becomes functionally outdated. Democracy and teamwork would become necessities of survival. We have not arrived at the point where bureaucracy is being eliminated but we are at a point where its existence is being questioned.

2

My main interest here is not the internal management problems of GM or Exxon, but the relation of bureaucracy to society. Partly because of its business success and partly because of the absence of a strong competitor, bureaucracy became the way to run nearly every organization and group. One finds bureaucracy almost everywhere, with the result that supposedly diverse areas of life tend to look alike. Rather than a "military-industrial complex" there seems to be a complex of government-industry-military-universities-churches-sports-entertainment. The "power elite" that C. Wright Mills described has reality in the very idea of "administrator." The head of an oil company can easily move into a presidential cabinet post. Not surprisingly, the commissioner of baseball comes to resemble a bishop. In this regard it may be noted in passing that the Christian church is only too relevant to the times.

Whatever one thinks of particular business conglomerates or the bureaucratic procedures of Catholic marriage tribunals, nearly everyone senses some danger in the growth of a single all-enveloping bureaucracy. Individuals rightly fear the concentration of too much power anywhere, even should the current holders of power seem to be benign in their disposition of it. There is great danger that at some point individuals may pass over to a state of helplessness, either resigning their fate to their masters or else striking out violently at social forms in their vicinity. In the pessimistic vision of Max Weber, the advancing "rationality" of the bureaucratic machine becomes a nightmare of irrationality for the individual.[5] Franz Kafka foresaw the vision and numerous twentieth century artists have filled in examples.

Without a counter-force, therefore, society can become one enormous "mega-machine." Once the conditions were right and the first steps had been taken in that direction, an inertial force continued the development. A deficiency of social models and a failure to develop other relationships are as much the cause of social injustice as a conspiracy on the part of a few or force against the many. "Society" does have a reality, an element of impersonality beyond the individuals who compose it. Nonetheless, in assigning responsibility for failure, we refer not to a thing called society or even an elite but to all the people who are related as society.

Society, therefore, includes each one of us. To the extent that *it* (the current pattern) is serving an individual then that individual has some vested interest in preserving the status quo. If the United States has 6 percent of the world's population and 50 percent of the goods, then that group has an inevitable tendency to perpetuate the same general arrangement. The individuals of that group are not the main cause of the disproportion, but just by acting "reasonably" they can maintain the same pattern. Here is the point at which the apparently neutral pattern of organizing work can be unjust because it is the means for perpetuating rank injustice.

Without firing a shot bureaucracy can ruthlessly carry the day. George Simmel wrote: "The essence of bureaucracies is the use to which they are put; these impersonal structures are corrupting only when they are taken as ends in themselves, when the processes by which they work most efficiently are taken to be an image of how society itself ought to function." [6] Simmel may be right but one should not underestimate how strong is the drive for this latter case to occur. The drift, in fact, is inevitable unless there are specific and effective human forces to stimulate society's search for a more just society. An unleashing of such power need not mean the disenfranchisement of anyone (though it would probably mean less quantity of goods for some). Certain sources have to be tapped if there is to be available a kind of power which is different from bureaucratic power. These three sources of power I am citing are education, religion and community. I could cite others (e.g., art) but these three are, at the least, good examples, and if properly developed they might include others.

My thesis is that society, especially in a bureaucratic pattern, resists those changes that can be defined as "humanizing," that is, change which dramatically reforms society as a whole in the direction of redistributing the means to live. Society prevents that kind of change from occurring by controlling the sources of that kind of change. Society controls the sources by the way in which it speaks about them. No guns are needed if one knows how to speak about education, community and religion in a way that neutralizes their effects.

What may seem to be the obvious control, namely, elimination, is almost never used. A country that outlaws religion probably does not know what it is doing, and almost certainly the move will not succeed. A challenge of that kind is likely to cause a reaction which would lead some people to get more serious about religion than ever before. Besides, as I have indicated, total elimination of these sources would, if successful, stop the game. Society finds a problem with passion and freedom but society knows that it cannot do without them. The question, therefore, is not to eliminate but to control community, education and religion.

The first mode of control is simply the blurring of language. In a casual if not thoughtless way the words community, education and religion float loose from any moorings. Everything in society becomes vaguely religious, vaguely communal, vaguely educational. What vaguely applies everywhere is not effectively present anywhere. The inflation of language is a most subtle way of destruction. One takes a powerfully laden word, overuses it in appropriate places and extends it to inappropriate applications. The result is that the word is evacuated of meaning.

The word community when used in every racial, school,

neighborhood and international dispute becomes a word to stick in when appealing for a hidden emotional response. The process is self-destructive because a word used in this way quickly loses any emotional sense and becomes a mere marker to take up space in sentences. At that point a government can refer to its spies as the "intelligence community" and no one laughs or cries. The emotional punch is gone and all that remains is the cover of respectability.

This way of controlling community, education and religion by devaluing the words through inflation has become more effective with modern advertising and TV news. There are so many words repeated in so many standard phrases that the words are no longer exchanges between human beings. When communication is sought, then words may not be trustworthy and we are forced into using inarticulate grunts. A recent book celebrates the emergence of a "whole new complex of interlocking clichés" as a sign of great progress. "The new consciousness has achieved a simplified, a swifter and more economical means of communication, ridding itself of the need for laborious explanations, tortuous literate communication, and cumbersome attention to detail." [7] One might hope that such cheery optimism has some foundation in reality but the statement reads like a bizarre parody of a government communiqué in a dystopian novel.

The blurring of language has a continuing function in the control of community, education and religion. This means is necessary but not sufficient. If everything is simply left vague there is always the danger that something real may coagulate. No matter that speech seems to have been reduced to the patter of clichés and that the human beings seem passively submissive to their fate. Time is no guarantee that human stubbornness has been eliminated, the stubbornness of a man or woman who on one day at one moment says: no. There is always the danger that underneath some floorboard hides Dostoyevsky's *Man From Underground* who reappears after forty years to declare that his life may be ridiculous but it is not the extracting of square roots.

3

The second and most efficient way to deal with the unpredictably human is to domesticate it. If community, education and religion must be allowed to exist, they cannot be allowed to roam. They are therefore tolerated and indeed encouraged to exist so long as they keep within their own confines. Those confines are the clearly defined interstices of the bureaucratic society that licenses their existence.

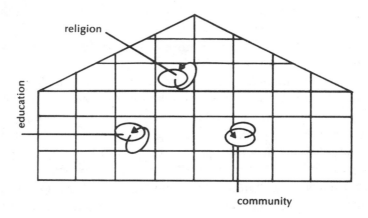

The chief demand upon these three little pockets is that each should be "reasonable." What could be more reasonable than a demand for reasonableness? However, reasonableness does not refer to the inner logic of the three concerns but to reason as conceived by the bureaucracy. The conflict which ensues stems from the fact already mentioned, namely, that the individual person experiences the rational structure as massively irrational. A black woman in a ghetto, who refuses to abide by Roberts Rules of Order at a meeting of the housing authority, is doing the only thing that humanly makes sense to her. There is reason for her action. The chairman who expels her from the meeting is also acting reasonably. The main issue is not the personal conflict but the question of what power defines the logic inherent to the situation.

Education, community and religion are expected to produce good citizens but, given the logic of the bureaucracy, good becomes translated into conforming. This fact is usually covered with phrases that assert almost the opposite (uniqueness, creativity, self-assertiveness). Beyond the high-flown rhetoric of educational writing, the fashioning of well-behaved citizens is the reasonable goal of education. Emile Durkheim was perhaps only too accurate in his description of what education actually does: "Education is the influence exercised by adult generations on those that are not yet ready for social life. . . . Education, far from having as its unique or principal object the individual and his interests, is above all the means by which society perpetually recreates the conditions of its very existence." [8]

The same kind of expectation surrounds both religion and community. Everyone knows what it means to be a "respectable member of the community." Likewise, it is assumed that a little religion (the noncontroversial kind) is essential for producing good citizens. "Civic religion" as it came to be known in the twentieth century has a long history in the United States.[9] On a visit to the country in 1860, Anthony Trollope noted that "everybody is bound to have a religion, but it does not matter what it is."

There is another carefully controlled variation on this theme. Since community, education and religion do keep insisting on their own logic, it is sometimes safer to give them their own little spaces for "experiments." Almost any strange thing may be done intramurally so long as it does not interfere with the main business of society. If the experiment spills over into the economic and political world, then it is only reasonable to curb it. Thus, if a group wishes to have a community in upper New Mexico or the Green Mountains there will probably be no opposition. The leaders of society can congratulate themselves on their tolerance and understanding. At the same time the power to work any change in the massive system of concentrated power is siphoned off. Everyone is thereby contented, both those who have kept control of things with a minimum of force and those who are playing out their rebelliousness while assuming they have escaped control.[10]

In this example one should not close the door prematurely. Society may miscalculate the nature of the threat. A revolution may someday come down from the mountains or up from the desert. Most educational, communal and religious movements do have their moments at the top of a mountain or out in the desert. But the moment was just that, a staging ground and not an end point.

What does not bode well in the current instance is the shift in the meaning of the word "commune." This word once carried powerful emotional and historical meaning. The commune was that form of community that arose in the midst of revolution and struck with decisive political action. Nothing would be more subversive of an unjust social order than the rise of the commune. But such communes can no longer arise when with blinding speed and extraordinary efficiency the word commune has had its meaning reversed. In the late 1960s commune took on a meaning that is antiurban, antimodern, antitechnological; in short, commune became an apolitical if not antipolitical word. Whatever happens from now on in Harlem or Watts,

Chicago or Washington, cannot be called a commune, and whatever it is called it will be lacking the historical power of a word now safely domesticated.

The problem is that those who want radical change do not usually realize how much their own attitudes are entwined in the very things they are attacking. Most of all their speech betrays them. Their cries for a changed order may be overlaid with a deposit of deadly metaphors implying inhuman control. The rebel often disregards accuracy of speech or else chooses images which are the counter-images of the order being attacked.

A pertinent example is the recent stress on consciousness in the drug revolution and elsewhere. The use of drugs to "expand consciousness" unwittingly played into the very controls from which the revolution was seeking to escape. As Juliet Mitchell points out, manipulative advertising has always been an expansion of consciousness.[11] No one is more at the mercy of political control than an individual with swollen or drugged consciousness. Consciousness fits neatly into bureaucratic interstices; of itself consciousness does nothing to alter these controls. To the extent that increased awareness gives us the illusion of being economically and politically freed, it worsens the social split of mind and body and increases institutional dominations.

Mitchell is concerned with the metaphors currently operating in the feminist movement. The phrase often used there is "consciousness raising" which changes the action but not the location of the metaphor. Possibly this is the best available metaphor but one cannot be too concerned with the limitations and implications of the chosen term. Robert Frost has written: "Great is he who imposes the metaphor." To which one might add that the metaphors are usually imposed by those who control the economic and political life of a society.

4

From the preceding description it is possible to decipher two principles by which society exercises the closest control of education, community and religion. These two principles are: (1) Identify each of these realities with a single institution. (2) Identify that institution with women and children. All of the various controls are easy to derive once these two principles are well established.

In the American language, community, education and religion are housed in their respective and separate places. It is almost impossible to distinguish each of these concerns from the single institution where each is presumed to belong. Thus, education is what takes place in school, religion is what goes on in church, and community is a family affair. That each of these concerns should have institutional expression is beyond debate. That there should be one and only one institution for each is neither necessary nor desirable. This point is crucial: it is not the institutionalization but the monopoly of institution that is undesirable. If that distinction is not made people end up fighting not only the wrong battle but a battle which worsens the problem they are trying to correct.

The problem is the common practice of interchanging education/school, religion/church, community/family. It may be objected that people can and do recognize the difference. The more relevant point is that in practice the distinction is overlooked or violated. Those who have control of the dominant institutions are not likely to protest against the preemption of the terms and those outside the institution are not likely to have the power or willingness to fight the linguistic battle.

First, there is the takeover of religion by church. The

framers of the U.S. Constitution forbade the "establishment of religion." They wished to avoid any one church
becoming an arm of the state, but they used the language
of the day in which religion equaled church. Church officials have not resisted this equivalence of religion and
church because it seemed to place the Christian church se-
curely in control of the entire area of religion. One result
is a long and confusing history of "church-state relations"
in the United States. Under this rubric fall questions of
civic and educational concern, like religion in public
education. "Church-state" is obviously a misleading phrase
in almost all the discussions. It hides the fact of the diversity of churches and more importantly it omits from religious discussion many people who have no part in any
church. The fact that the language is traditional does not
make it less confusing for all and less insulting to many.[12]

The takeover of education by school is one in which
schoolteachers and administrators willingly participate.
There are occasional references to education beyond the
walls or without the walls but that language does little to
shake the establishment of the school system. Even attacks under the artificial term "deschooling" are easily
absorbed within the system of control. The attacks often
exaggerate the importance of the school as controlling not
only education but the world. There is something puzzling,
as Maxine Greene points out, about the apparent maso-
chism of schoolteachers attacking school. "There is something titillating to a teacher's ego in becoming aware
that he, whose professionalism has so often been questioned, is a reluctant Atlas holding the system on his shoul-
ders." [13] As the religious traditions have warned, in back
of an exaggerated humility there often lurks a false pride.

It could be argued that in the case of the word education, that word should be relinquished to the school. One
could then distinguish, for example, learning and educa-

tion, with the word education here equivalent to the institution of school. Perhaps that would be an easier language to defend but I think it gives up too much. The word education, despite its reduction in many school circles, is still a rich word with connotations worth preserving. Education carries a sense of form and organization not found in the word learning.

The identification of the word community with the institution of family is the least evident of the three examples but it is nonetheless there. Although community is used in innumerable vague ways, the one thing which ties down American usage is mother, father and children. Usually there are several mother-father-children components but not more than could comfortably surround the town square in properly zoned houses. The apparent flexibility of the word community hides the rigidity of the family as a precisely and narrowly defined institution.

There has been considerable bewailing of the collapse of the home and the disintegration of the family. Actually, it is more likely that the family has been growing more powerful; that is, the institution of family has increased its hegemony over community. As Richard Sennett has noted: "The urban family of this affluent era has developed a power to absorb activities and interests that were once played out in a variety of settings in the city. Indeed, it might best be said of city life during the past twenty-five years of suburban growth that the scale of life has become too intimate, too intense." [14]

Sennett's concern is indicative of why all three of these institutional monopolies are corruptive. Every institution is of its nature conservative; humans express themselves in organized fashion to achieve continuity with others, including continuity with past generations. To conserve is a human good but human conserving is one that takes place in continually changing expressions. The forms change when there is interaction of forms which opens imagination to previously undreamt possibilities. Without outside criticism institutions become introverted, thereby ceasing to be properly conservative and becoming instead defensively reactionary. One sign of a monopolistic institution is that it has lost a sense of its *raison d'être* and is mainly intent on self-preservation.

If the charge of monopoly of form is correct then the answer is obvious: diversity of form. But one should note that this diversity will come about through two-pronged action: change within the current form complemented by attempts to establish alternate forms. To attack the existing institution is probably undesirable and almost certainly ineffective. To reform the existing institution is of value but taken in isolation could increase the repressiveness of that form. Only by both re-form and multiplying form do we have a way out of our difficulties.

Attacks upon church, family and school cannot possibly work. The attacks generate attention but little else. In the first place, it is doubtful that these three can die because they are so firmly entrenched. The family is of such a nature that it cannot cease. School may approach the same status and church is not far behind. Second, whether or not they can die, it is patently clear that all three are alive and massively powerful. There is nothing easier to discredit than a premature obituary. Everett Reimer's book carried the sensational title *School Is Dead*. If the title were *School is Deadening* it would be descriptive of some available experience. *School Is Dead* just happens to be factually dead wrong.[15]

The worst effect of supposedly radical assaults on the existence of family, church and school is that all three are left to pursue their paths unchecked by critical examination. Furthermore, those who try to eliminate these institutions are often expressing the alienated and destructive individualism which those monopolistic institutions engender. Overthrowing institutions would not suddenly free everyone but would only expose vulnerable individuals to chaos.

When the underlying attitude is antiinstitutional a cycle of frustration occurs. Whether the rebellion is communal, educational or religious the sequence reads: (1) Let's get free of the institution's control of us. (2) Why do we need an institution at all? Let's just all work together. (3) Why are things not working as beautifully as in the beginning? Let's agree on a minimum of rules. (4) Why are we swamped with rules and still can't get anywhere? Let's have a little more order. (5) Let's get free of all this.

The first necessity is re-form, that is, to make changes in existing forms. There are obvious improvements that can be made in the functioning of schools, churches and families. The work of patient reform is not to be belittled. If the inherent limitations of the institution are recognized then every little humanizing touch is to be applauded. The only danger, I have indicated, is a reform not accompanied by diversification. For example, a fervent church could turn out to be a menace. The attempt of church officials to restore the missionary spirit in *Key '73* was understandably feared by many Jews. The Jews had been over that route before with a church intent on its mission to save everyone. University officials who invite student reform of the school may intentionally or not be further extending the school's control of students, preventing them from getting an education, both in and out of school. Likewise, the family needs reform but not in the direction of introverted self-sufficiency.

5

The complement to reform is diversification of form. More comment is necessary on this issue. Sometimes reform and multiplication shade off into each other but there is something else clearly at stake in this latter word.

In education, much of the "radical school movement" has been an attempt to replace the existing school with an alternative school. But the same problems immediately reemerge: utopian aims, inflated rhetoric, a feeling of coercion and a takeover of the students' lives. An excellent article of a few years back by Fred Newmann and Donald Oliver proposed a threefold form for education: the school, the laboratory, the community seminar.[16] More recently, Theodore Sizer has written that we do not need an alternative school but rather alternative educational forms of which one might be the main elements of existing schools.[17] For discussing his proposal Sizer uses the terms academy (the existing school re-formed) and collegium (extracurricula and other educational experiences).[18] I doubt that the terms are adequate but the proposal of some language is needed to be able to talk of other educational institutions which are not schools. The other route of speaking of dramatically diverse forms of school is possible but is one I argued against in contrasting education and learning. There are some valuable elements in the traditional meaning of school and these can be preserved by releasing school from the burden of providing all education.

The case for a multiplicity of religious forms should be more obvious. Here it is less the invention of new forms so much as the recognition of them. We do not need more churches; probably we need fewer. Although churches do exist in the plural there is a legitimacy to the term Christian church. The singular is justified by the fact that the churches agree upon one thing, namely, that there is no serious religious competitor to the Christian church. Any institution that pretended to be a form comparable to the church had to be overcome. The Christian church sees itself as badly divided, but from the outside it is only too unified in its attitude toward the rest of the world. The attitude, it may be claimed, is changing, but skepticism about this fact is justified insofar as little change has occurred in basic speech patterns. In any case, members and officials of the Christian church could help by never referring to religion when in fact they mean church.

The word community needs more help than what can be achieved by reform of the family. It has only been in this century that family has come to mean "nuclear family," that is, mother, father and a decreasing number of children. However, the word is firmly lodged there so that to talk of other "familial" relations we now refer to "extended family." The return of grandfathers and aunts to the family circle might be a help to community though the recovery seems unlikely. In any case, the question of community is not reducible to the extended family.

The family even if extended would not be sufficient to supply all of the community experience that every individual desperately needs today. The big problem is to recover a variety of social relations that have been ruptured and possibly to invent some new ones. Community is the issue in architectural design, the legal profession, subway trains, health services, football games, drug use and hundreds of other places. The problem is so encompassing that it is difficult to know where to begin. Part of the beginning would be to use the word community in a comprehensive but consistent way. Community, as I shall elaborate in chapter four, refers to the specifically human way of relating. One form of this reality is the family; other forms need recognition, rediscovery, improvement or invention.

6

The first principle of bureaucratic control I have been describing is that community, education and religion are identified with a single institution. The plot thickens when we come to the other principle of control, namely, that institution is identified with women and children, or more precisely, with those assumed to be minors. Men are usually in charge of the institution but the real participants are women and children.

School is an institution which is controlled by men, run by women and provided for children. Church is an institution presided over by men but the real population of churches is women and children. Likewise, the community leader is the man but community exists where mommy and the kids are. Daddy comes home from work in what claims to be the real world so that he can be refreshed by community, that is, by the wife and children. There is much talk about a change in these three patterns but statistics do not seem to indicate much basic change.[19]

The significance of this identification is no great mystery. If community, education and religion are the provinces of helpless minors then no serious impetus for change can come from these sources. The rulers of society can speak in glowing terms of these institutions and go to great lengths in protecting the people in them. What the rulers are excused from doing is listening to suggestions that come from these little ones. "Aren't they cute?" Kindly and condescending humor is taken to be the appropriate response. As the feminist movement found, that kind of humor was the deadliest opponent it had to meet.

A feminist movement has achieved some degree of serious recognition but the movement is still only beginning. There is considerable scurrying to give a few women visible jobs in television, universities and politics. But any fundamental realignment of the institutions I am describing has hardly begun. Even with the best of will the change might take generations and the presence of goodwill is not yet to be presumed.

The problem which women face at this time is one that has been faced by other groups in similar movements, namely, whether to infiltrate one at a time or to work as a group from the outside. Getting a job in the male hierarchy gives one leverage to change the organization; it also exposes one to being absorbed by the organization. The women's movement was not a success on the day it got its first board member at General Motors. Success would be marked by the general realization that if there must be a GM, at least the rest of the world does not have to be an imitation.

The sexual caste structure of school, church and family represents an encroachment of the bureaucratic pattern into the very areas that are supposed to challenge bureaucracy. Originally, however, the opposite was the case. Bureaucracy arose in continuity with the paternalism already present in family, church and school. There has been a confusing circular motion here. Bureaucracy feeds from the worst (sexist) side of school, church and family but it then gets support by appealing to all the positive, nostalgic feelings for school, church and family.

In their turn school, church and family have never recognized what they gave birth to, thereby exposing themselves to a creeping bureaucracy of the worst sort. For example, universities are combinations of medieval monasteries and business conglomerates. Instead of places where teachers teach students, universities function as enormous administrative superstructures to which are attached teachers (often hard to find) and plenty of consumers. The confusion of form together with misleading rhetoric makes the university one of the worst bureaucracies in the country. Its only serious competition may be the church, whose self-descriptions can also be misleading. While pretending not to be a bureaucracy the church carelessly acquires some of the worst trappings of bureaucracy with the result that the church has the procedures but not the efficiency of a bureaucratic institution. The fact that the family is an inept bureaucracy is hidden by the smallness of each operation. But if one projects all those "housewives" doing what they are supposed to do with the latest labor-saving devices, one would wonder if there were not possible a better arrangement of time, energy and people.

7

If the analysis of the problem is correct, that school, church and family are reserved for women and children, what is the solution to the problem? The answer must ultimately be to get some men and/or adults involved. However, the short-term tactics for working toward this goal remain debatable. The absence of men is not an accident that could be rectified by a little advertising. In a hierarchical pattern almost no man will choose to be on the bottom if he can help it. One must change the pattern by getting a large group of men at the bottom or a large group of women at the top. What could then occur would be the end of tops and bottoms. Just as it is questionable to get a few women at the top so it is of doubt-

ful value to get a few men at the bottom. The presence
of a few men might be a step forward but this is not certain. One must reckon today with the new possibilities of
woman power. Sisterhood may be a more powerful lever
than male tokenism.

Whatever the immediate steps, the long-range goal
is clear: education, community and religion becoming
adult concerns. To be fully adult they would have to be
a fairly even mixture of men and women. If men do not
now come in significant numbers, women can still insist
on being treated like adults rather than minors. As it is
now, the participants are assumed to be children who need
protection and control. In education, for example, the
words child and student function interchangeably. Although "adult education" is widely discussed today, the
term itself indicates that it is a coda to the enormous educational bureaucracy. A person who wishes to have some
formal education throughout life is still thought to be a
little strange.

We should note that school is a place particularly appropriate for children. Childhood is the apt time for
acquiring basic tools of reading, writing and arithmetic.
Adult learning ought to have a different form which would
not be called school. The special relation that education
has to children is one which is shared by community and
religion. All three of them are concerned with the survival and growth of the race of humans. The test of that
concern is what they do with little children and old
people, the links to past and future generations. A society that is apparently overconcerned with these groups
is very likely exercising a false concern. Children and old
people are not best cared for by placing them into institutions segregated from the rest of life. If society were
really interested in the education of children, it would

show more care for the nine months before birth and the first couple of years after birth.

A child-centered world is not a human world because it is a misleading and artificial world. Children need something to grow up *into*. In the available forms of education, community and religion, everything is sacrificed for the children, which is not healthy for the children, let alone the nonchildren. The children would have a better chance of growing if there were an adult-centered society in which they were at first minor participants and only later full-fledged members.

Institutions which are set up to take care of helpless minors have a double edge to them. The protection tends to become overextended and the rhetoric grossly inflated. Church, family and school are talked about as if they were the cure for every social problem. Even when it becomes clear that they are not solving the problem, it is assumed that there has been a minor breakdown which can be rectified with a few pieties. Almost everyone senses an enormous gap between the pretentious language and the actual institution but the admission that there is something structurally wrong does not surface easily.

An example of the difficulty in this area was the book *Inequality* written by Christopher Jencks and associates in 1972.[20] The book was simply and clearly written and was backed with careful research; the book was also received with considerable coolness. Jencks's conclusion was that the school has not been and cannot be the main instrument for achieving social equality. The book brought painfully up-to-date the findings of several "revisionist" histories of nineteenth century education, namely, that the school exacerbated rather than solved the problem of inequality. A bureaucratic school system cannot equalize classes because bureaucracy itself is a class structure.[21]

The inability of the system to deal in any effective way with the problem does not prevent the system from making ambitious claims for itself and accepting impossible tasks. Jencks, agreeing with Ivan Illich's characterization of school as today's secular church, explains why the school is loaded with extravagant claims and unrealistic expectations: "A religion which promises anything less than salvation wins few converts. In school, as in church, we deal with the world that we wish existed, trying to inspire our descendents with ideals we ourselves have failed to live up to. We assume, for example, that there is no chance of making adults live together in desegregated neighborhoods, so we try to impose this ideal on children by inventing elaborate school busing plans." [22] If school had a more limited aim and worked in conjunction with other institutions, it might contribute to an amelioration of social inequities.

In summary, society (or those with proportionate vested interest in a bureaucratic and hierarchic society) resists any change in the distribution of power, status and possessions. Three forces that pose a threat to society's machinelike working are community, education and religion. None of the three can be eliminated (or else the price is too high) but the three can be segregated from each other and confined to safe reservations. Each of them is given a nice place to live and the inhabitants are provided with elaborate security and protection. The inmates are women, children and men who are presumably childish or effeminate. For their special privileges and protection, as well as for the lavish praise they receive on appropriate occasions, they should be grateful and not rebel against the devices provided for their safety. With community, education and religion neatly domesticated within the interstices of society, society can get on with its serious business.

If the description of the problem is accurate, then the

direction of social reform is patently clear: (1) It must challenge the institutional monopoly and isomorphism of school, family, church. (2) It must desegregate, especially by sex and age, the island populations of community, religion and education. (3) It must finally—and this would be the sign of progress—bring about intersections of community, education and religion. Every breaking through of the segregating walls is a step forward but the linguistic change has to accompany institutional attempts. If community, education and religion should discover each other there would be a dramatic power reversal. All the energy that is now directed toward repressing the body and controlling the individual would be redirected toward life, love and growth.

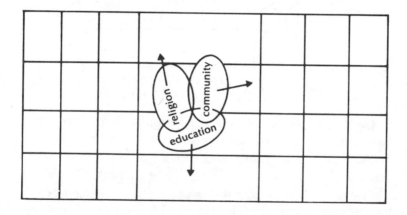

8

All of the preceding description of this chapter has been a preface to the statement of my main thesis: To the extent that the Christian church accepts the identification of religion and church, the church tends to mirror the same pattern of community and education found in the larger society. This thesis implies: (1) that religious education and religious community in the church will be segregated into isolated reservations; (2) that religious education and religious community will each be totally identified with one institution; (3) that that institution will be identified with women and children; (4) that the purpose of these two institutions will be conformity to the church so that the church can get on with its business.

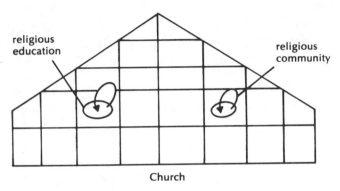

religious education

religious community

Church

Getting at the source of this problem in the church is more difficult than in society as a whole. Society too narrowly defines community and education but presumably it has the right to do the defining. The extraordinary thing about the church's definitions of religious education and religious community is the assumption that the church has the right to do the defining. Unless this presumption is challenged then all reforms of religious education and religious community in the church may add to the arrogance of the church's position.

The church's assumption of this right follows, of course, from society assigning religion to church. But this fact raises the question of why the church accepted the role assigned to it. Why did a church which loudly proclaims its independence and critical function allow itself to be safely domesticated by modern society?

Much of the answer to this question has already been suggested. The Christian church was from the start vulnerable in its claim to have a final solution for everyone. The structural problems related to such a claim could probably not have been solved in the early church; in any case they were not. There was no communal/sexual revolution accompanying the Christian movement. Neither was there an educational development that would be adequate for a worldwide religious body. It can be argued that the Christian movement did have some good effects both sexually and educationally. Nevertheless, the church almost immediately began a division into a class structure along sexual and educational lines.

At the beginning of modern times the church was well formed as a paternalistic organization. What should have been viewed as its worst weakness could easily be viewed as a virtue with the rise of the bureaucratic state and technological organization. The church was implicitly asked whether it wished to be eliminated or else to conform to the one organizational pattern which was henceforth acceptable. The church readily accepted the deal because it meant the continuation of real though reduced power for the church. Perhaps, more exactly, it was power for the paternalistic church elite who had become accustomed to dealing with heads of state.

Western society allowed the churches to exist and in most places churches were actively supported by governments. All control of religion was placed in the guardianship of the church, either one denomination or one generalized church. Other gifts, like tax exemptions, accompanied the major gift of monopoly of religious life. In return, the church had only to promise to produce good citizens, those who would uphold society's arrangements.

Patriotism and religion became nearly inseparable and they were the peculiar loves of country and of God arranged for in a bureaucratic church.

In hindsight it is easy to see that for every tax-exempt dollar and draft-exempt clergyman the church paid with a piece of life. It would be unkind and unfair to be too critical of men who acted to save their church. One might speculate that there should have been more resistance by the church to the role assigned it. The resistance was mostly among scattered individuals.

The reason for raising the issue is not to heap accusations or blame on past generations. The fact is, however, that that church is still with us speaking a language of the sixteenth century. The illusions of language continue in ecclesiastical leaders of today. Even progressive theology of the contemporary church seems oblivious to the fact that the church is a demonstration of what theology often attacks. I will return to this question of theology and bureaucratic church in the next chapter.

9

We can now note how the Christian church uses its assumed right to speak about religious community and religious education. The language of religious community is clearer in Catholic than Protestant churches. Also, there are differences between Catholic and Protestant in their language of religious education. However, there is no fundamental difference in the communal and educational operations.

In the Roman Catholic church the term religious community is equivalent to one peculiar institutionalization of religious community, namely, the canonical religious order/congregation. In both official and popular Catholic language there is no distinction made between the terms religious community and religious order. The problem is further complicated by Catholic usage of the phrase "the religious life." This phrase represents the ultimate in co-option. By referring to itself this way the institution takes over all religious organization and life as well, without even the admission that it is itself an organization. Compared to this organization, every other form of life is by definition irreligious or nonreligious. The most remarkable implication of this language is that priests, bishops and popes do not lead "the religious life."

There is no accident in the church's use of this strange, ancient language. The kind of religion which can be totally appropriated by the church is the religion practiced by the most conforming members of the church. The chief virtue of the people in these organizations has always been considered to be obedience. Lavish praise is bestowed upon "the religious" for doing the work of the church in obedience to the bishops and popes. Church authorities believe that their right and their duty is to exercise total control over "religious communities." Generally, there is little interference in internal matters but whenever a problem emerges to the outside world it is likely to bring in priests or bishops to correct the situation.

In this clearest case of the Catholic meaning of religious community, the second principle of control is powerfully operative. That is, the term "religious community" is female. When the term "religious community" is used it is nearly always assumed that the reference is to a group of women. The phrase "priests and religious" is simply another form of "priests and nuns." There does exist the anomaly of men in religious orders but for all practical purposes this fact is denied. Either the man becomes a priest in one of the orders (thus ceasing to be part of a community and becoming an "order priest") or else it is assumed he could not make the grade and needs taking care of like a nun. I have said that children are usually associated with community and the absence of children in Catholic "religious communities" puts some strain on the language. However, nuns are generally associated with taking care of children and have been treated as children even more than have other women.

Catholic and Protestant parishes are reduced versions of the meaning of "religious community." The isomorphism is almost total; the geographical district is the norm for the community. The parish is almost invariably run by a man though the workers and listeners are mostly women and children. The relation of pastor to flock is similar to that of prior to monks or mother superior to nuns. The obedience demanded on ecclesiastical matters is complete. There is, of course, acknowledgment that the parish members have to be allowed their "secular" lives. Some controlled sex is allowable somewhere other than in church, legitimated particularly if it is to produce new church members. Some material possessions are allowable, particularly if a good part of them is given to support the church. But freedom, sex and goods of the earth remain highly suspect. Parish life remains a limited version of the real meaning of "religious community."

In the language of religious education in church the same two principles of control appear. First, religious education is domesticated in a single institution. Second, that institution is identified with women and children.

In the U.S. Catholic church the task of religious education belonged to the Catholic school and what is to this day an imitation Catholic school, namely, the Confraternity of Christian Doctrine (*CCD*). Under extreme financial pressure the system has been rapidly changing but it is not clear that any overhaul of organizational thinking has occurred. What emerges as new organization could be a combination of Catholic school/nun reduced to the lowest possible limit and a Protestant system that has not been notably successful. I refer to the "parish coordinator" movement which has spread across the U.S. Catholic church since about 1967. There is the possibility that in the parish coordinator the Catholic church may get more than it is looking for. The movement hangs in the balance: It either is the avant-garde of a total church change or else a reenforcement of stereotyped "religious education."

U.S. Protestant efforts to isolate and neutralize religious education have usually worked through Sunday school. The Sunday school was intended to be the complement of the public school which functioned during the week. In the weekday school, children were to learn the nonsectarian religion of America while Sunday was to convince them to become practicing members of their denomination. Sunday school has its difficulties today but the significance of this fact should not be exaggerated; it has always been in trouble. Robert Lynn and Elliot Wright in *Big Little School* have documented the depressing history of the Sunday school. Amazingly, they end with no particular hope of change.

> A study in the mid-decades of the twentieth century indicated that pastors spent less than 5 percent of their time on the educational work of the church or "little more than they have to give to janitorial services." Aside from the fact that it is a rare clergyman in the 1970's who wields a broom, the data is probably still reliable. Scores upon scores of Sunday schools in urban and rural areas function, as they always have, in relative separation from the rest of the church. "Sunday school is Sunday school" and "Church is

Church" and in Western Nebraska and on Tennessee's Cumberland Plateau one can skip the latter but not the former if social respectability is to be maintained. Given the tensions which have existed between Sunday school and congregation, superintendent and pastor, it is somewhat amazing that the educational program has survived at all.[23]

As for the conclusion in the last sentence of this quotation, it is indeed amazing: (1) that the authors should be surprised that the Sunday school continues; (2) that they can assume that what goes on can be called an educational program. There is nothing at all surprising about the survival of the Sunday school. The conflict of ideals and the 5 percent of clergy time fit in perfectly with the system. The Sunday school was precisely the place to deposit grand ideals out of sight of the church. How else could the contemporary church exist without such a training and feeder system? If Sunday school ceased to exist the church would have to invent something similar. What would really be surprising would be programs that really were *educational*. Neither Lynn-Wright's book nor other evidence suggests that the Sunday school has a clear right to assume the term educational.

The Catholic and Protestant institutions of religious education have been places for women and children. This identification has probably been even stronger in church than in the wider society. Little children go to Catholic school, CCD or Sunday school and the teachers are almost invariably women. Traditionally, the women have been unprepared for the work and the lack of preparation was part of the system, not an aberration in it. A competent staff of teachers would pose a threat to the objective of the traditional church school. The ecclesiastical conception

of education has been a combination of controlled orthodoxy and emotional appeal. The pastor need only
devote 5 percent of his time to this concern because he
has the final say on what is already an established system
of procedures and answers.

Religious education in the Christian church is a term
for women and children. When adults (translated men)
study religion it is called something else, usually theology.
Catholic and Protestant seminaries have traditionally had
a course on religious education. The course was kept separate from the serious work of theology, entering the seminary not as education but as a minor branch of "pastoral
theology." Religious education in seminaries did not pertain to the religious education of seminarians. It prepared
the future priest or minister to run a program for his congregation, that is, how to direct his directress of religious
education. Not surprisingly, this was the course that
women taught in seminaries.

10

The strategy for dealing with this inadequate church structure parallels the general strategy of social change cited
earlier in this chapter. There will not be progress unless
the stranglehold of language is broken. Religious education and religious community have to be freed in meaning
from their severe institutional restriction in the Christian
church. That redefinition is the work of chapters four
and five in this book.

As for institutional reform, the needs are clear: (1) diversification of form for religious education and religious
community; (2) the involvement of men and/or adults
in the area of religious education and religious commu-

nity; (3) the intersection of the two areas of religious education and religious community.

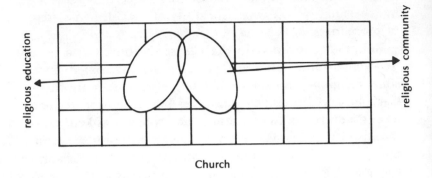

At present the literature on religious education has almost nothing to do with literature on religious community.
If there were re-form accompanied by multiplication of
form the two areas would expand until they broke the wall
between them. As they intersect a reversal of energy would
occur so that the Christian church would begin changing
in the direction of religious community-education. The
ideal, therefore, is not simply expansion of meaning so that
religious education and religious community are as large
as church. What needs to happen is a near reversal of
meaning so that religious education and religious community are much larger than church.

The tactic of getting men involved in these areas of
church remains questionable, just as in the larger society.
A typical lecture or religious education course in the
church will draw 70 to 90 percent women. Efforts should
probably be made to attract more men. Certainly, the
presence of men among the Catholic parish coordinators
shakes up the old stereotypes and gives the movement
more hope than it would otherwise have. In general, however, groups of women may hold the key to church reform.

The church may unintentionally become one of the staging grounds for the feminist revolution. The many women associated with religious education and religious community may discover a new power and new identity.

Before proceeding with religious education and religious community it is necessary to look at the adjective in each. The church forms of religious education and religious community are indicative of the operative meaning of "religious" for the Christian church. Breaking the isomorphism of religious community and religious education requires breaking the identification of Christian and religious. Only within an ecumenical religious dialogue can the church change its attitudes and thereby reform its own internal structure.

Chapter Three

The Religious Phenomenon

The previous two chapters have indicated the problematic character of religion in human life. Religion tends to go bad if it comes under the control of rulers who use it for their own purposes. In modern times this control has taken the form of religion becoming the ideology of a bureaucratic class structure. The individual is placed at the mercy of external forces and may face a life of extreme passivity.

My interest here as elsewhere is to describe what is happening religiously and to offer a language that is adequate to the phenomenon. I will do this in large part by examining the categories of faith and revelation to bring out the ambiguities of the word religion. Rebellion against old forms of religion does not necessarily free one from the negative side of religion. What is needed is a way of speaking that would reveal the ambivalence of religion.

Religion, more than politics, business and education, seems to stand in severe tension with every form of organization. However, the notion of religion already includes some organization. Phrases like "organized religion" or "institutional religion" verge on redundancy. The place to begin a contrast is not between organized and nonorganized religion. Rather, one should be attentive to the difference between religion and religious, the noun being an abstraction while the adjective can refer to a positive component in the life of an individual, group or organization. The important questions here are: (1) What is the relation between the noun religion and the adjective religious? (2) What nouns follow the adjective religious?

This chapter deals mostly with the noun religion, an inquiry it should be admitted that is legitimate though possibly misleading. Human life exists in forms which acquire a status of their own capable of being studied. Religious life has forms which can be generalized into an abstract notion called religion. George Santayana was correct in saying that one can no more have religion in general than one can speak language in general. Nonetheless, one can study language and one can also study religion. My intention is to make some generalizations about religion as a prelude to placing the question in the proper context of religious education, religious community and religious body.

Almost everyone has now heard that some kind of sizable religious movement is afoot in the United States. The movement may or may not be regressive but in either case it is a surprise to those who had predicted the elimination of religion. According to the scheme of Auguste Comte, religion and all forms of mystery and magic should have disappeared in the advancing enlightenment. The last step along that path, still expected a few years ago, has not occurred and a dramatic reversal seems to have been set in motion.

The eighteenth century had trusted in the power of common sense and empirical science to dissolve the mystifications of religion. Karl Marx was more perceptive in his recognition that the role which religion played precluded its being dissolved by common sense or empirical science. One has to dig underneath things to unearth the instrumental purposes of religion. In the struggle for a better society, Marx identified religion as the chief enemy: "The critique of religion is the presupposition of all critique. . . . The foundation of irreligious critique is this: Man makes religion, religion does not make man. Indeed, religion is man's self-consciousness and self-awareness insofar as he has either not yet found himself or has lost himself again." [1]

Both the eighteenth century call for light and the Marxist call for the overturning of religion are still with us today. The contribution of both attitudes is considerable but so is the deficiency of each. Part of the trouble lay in the almost total identification of religion and the modern Western church. There was practically no way to ask a nonecclesiastical religious question. Fighting against religion when their main enemy was the church easily led the opponents of religion to overkill and to attacking what is inherently human.

Alfred North Whitehead provides a sympathetic yet very critical summary of the eighteenth century attitude:

> It was the age of reason, healthy, manly, upstanding reason; but, of one-eyed reason, deficient in its vision of depth. We cannot overrate the debt of gratitude which we owe to these men. For a thousand years Europe had been a prey to intolerant, intolerable visionaries. The common sense of the eighteenth century, its grasp of the obvious facts of human suffering, and of the obvious demands of human nature, acted on the world like a bath of moral cleansing. . . . But if men cannot live on bread alone, still less can they do so on disinfectants.[2]

Reason was now capable of removing the restraints which Christianity had brought upon the world but it was not clear who or what would set new limits. And without some agreements and restraints it has become increasingly clear that men and women cannot live together on the earth.[3]

The nineteenth century critique by Marx was more profound but it has not itself escaped later criticism. Churchmen have endlessly attacked Marx but the more interesting thing is a criticism of Marx's religious critique by those who are sympathetic to Marx. The statement quoted above that "man makes religion, religion does not make man" is peculiarly abstract and surprisingly non-dialectical. All three words, man, makes and religion, are abstractions which are inadequate to the topic in question. In other places, Marx does recognize the dialectical character of religion as when he writes that "religious suffering is at the same time an expression of real suffering and a protest against real suffering." In passing from the abstraction *religion* to multiple and ambivalent forms of *religious* suffering and *religious* protest, the way is opened even within Marxism to new possibilities.[4] In the course of his book which praises, defends and reinterprets Marx, Michael Harrington can still write: "It may well be, in contrast to what Marx thought, that once man stops dying from famines and poverty and starts to die only from death, there will be a resurgence of the religious spirit, not an end to it." [5]

Perhaps this comment of Harrington's explains some of what has been happening in the twentieth century. Having solved many of the technical problems that had fascinated them, some people in the technologically advanced world seem to be coming full circle. Religion seems to be back in style. This resurgence of the religious element is probably in part antitechnological and in part posttechnological. In either case, a new concern for some simple and perennial human questions has come back to center stage. From the position of only recently having been judged irrelevant, religion seems suddenly to have become a very appropriate concern. "What we call religion directs itself, at least at best, to precisely the kinds of altered relationships to death and the continuity of life that occur during any historical turning point." [6]

The resurgence of religion may indicate the incapacity of society to deal with its problems. But the fact of the resurgence is also evidence that in times of great trauma some form of religion is bound to emerge. What Gordon Allport wrote of individual patients might be applied to society as a whole. Allport challenged the assumption that the presence of religion in disturbed patients means that religion caused the breakdown. "It may well turn out," he wrote, "that preoccupation with religion was not the cause but the *effect* of the breakdown. What language other than religion can represent to a disturbed patient the mysterious forces that he feels?" [7]

What kind of "new religion" is emerging out of the explosion of religious elements is difficult to say. There is not an adequate framework and language in which to study the development. A "scientific study of religion" has existed for over a century and a field of "Christian theology" has been with us for many centuries but there has not been an integration of these two. Christian theology goes its own way unaffected in its basic premise by the rise of the study of religion. Logically, one would expect the field of religious study to establish the premises and Christian theology to be subsumed within that context. That logical route may not be the realistic one; at least right now there are two obstacles.

First, Christian theology, though a minority voice in the world, dominates religious discourse in the Western, technological world. The language of Christian theology is the verbal reflection of most religious organizations in the United States. That language must be broken through if religious organization is to change. An attempt simply to put aside the language of Christian theology would prove illusory.

Second, the study of religion in the West reflects its origin and its position as an alternative to Christian theology, not a broader field ready to incorporate Christian theology. Some people began in the field of religion with an antichurch attitude. Others have been adherents of the Christian church who had to put aside their Christian beliefs to study strange new things in other worlds. Undoubtedly there has been progress here but the subjective component in all religion still poses a methodological problem for the study of religion.

2

I wish to approach this problem through examining the concept and word revelation. In a previous book I have set out a proposal for defining the word revelation.[8] My reason for choosing this word is the claim that revelation may be the most helpful category to open dialogue between the religious and the not-religious, the Christian and not-Christian, the human and the not-human aspects of experience. My negative reason for examining revelation is that its traditional and continuing role is to hide the arrogant claim on which Christian theology is based. If the premise of a "Christian revelation" is not removed, then there is still an obstruction to serious dialogue.

This consideration of revelation pertains to material within Christian theology but is not part of Christian theology. The term theology itself is of doubtful salvageability because of the claim inherent to the word. My comments would fall within a philosophy of religion but I am not abiding by the rules often assumed by philosophers who are church members. These philosophers would seem to be at least as negligent as theologians in failing to examine the intelligibility of the concept of revelation. Theologians might be excused for not wishing to tamper with the premise that gives them existence; philosophers are not supposed to leave any domain untouched.

The philosophers who deal with these matters almost invariably reflect upon "faith," a category which I shall claim cannot capture the religious phenomenon. The philosophical examination of faith as a subjective attitude of openness and trust only worsens the problem of a Christian theology. Philosophy deferentially stops at the claim of a "Christian revelation" leaving this unintelligible concept nowhere to go except outside the believer's head. Placing this something somewhere back in history does not make it more intelligible but it does serve to obscure the claim. If one can believe that somewhere, somehow God deposited with the Christian church something called a revelation, then the believer has only minor problems after that.

Liberal Christian theology blurs what things are supposed to be in that revelation but the claim to have a revelation functions as imperiously as it does in conservative Christian theology. For example, Heinz Zahrnt's *What Kind of God?* claims to be radically critical of Christian theology. Yet, the author can write:

> If we look at both experiences together, our experience of the world and our experience when we encounter the reality of revelation, can we then recognize that there is a "surplus" contained in the truth of the revelation of God? This surplus consists in the manifestation of the fact, which it is impossible to derive from any experience of the world, that the final and absolute power over our existence is that of love.[9]

Even after granting allowance for the ambiguity of several key words and the translation from German, is there any sense at all to such statements? What does the word revelation actually refer to here, a surplus that cannot be derived from any experience of the world? The best guess is that he is talking about someone reading the Christian scriptures. How anyone finds there the final explanation of life is not explained. Why the belief in this fact is never subjected to liberal criticism is even more incomprehensible. One thing sure is that the possibility of dialogue is severely reduced with anyone who has a final answer like that in hand.

A conservative Christian theologian who believes that the church had the truth dictated to it around the year 30 will listen to no critique. Submitting the "Word of God" to philosophical examination can only be considered blasphemy. But liberal Christian theology admits to criteria for intelligibility in human discourse. If the word revelation no longer means what it does in fundamentalism, then it is legitimate to ask what definite meaning it does have.

Philosophy that emerges near or within the Christian church could contribute to a clarification by raising the challenge rather than shying away. Reverence and humility may be admirable qualities in a philosopher of religion but they are not a substitution for philosophical criticism. From many examples, I will cite two recent works that are impressive for their size, ambition and scholarship.

Wilfred Desan has a major work entitled *Planetary Man*. In the introduction to two volumes published together, the author states:

> The center around which our integration is built is not a supernatural one. This is a philosophical work, and although the possibility of revelation is not excluded, it is viewed as not relevant here. Man may

indeed belong to the sphere of the sacred, as some claim, but this consideration has no place in our philosophical research. This is an attempt of man on his own, and the dialectic unrolls without the help of revelation, as far as it goes. Some may think it does not go far enough. This is not the philosopher's fault. His world is autonomous but not complete.[10]

Aside from the fact that the author does not seem to abide by this statement (e.g., pages 129, 160, 365), the statement itself is a peculiar philosophical credo. Is not the claim to a revelation and the intelligibility of such a claim open to philosophical questioning? Why should a philosopher's world be incomplete when everything available in the world is open to analysis? The use of the word supernatural is a strange one for a philosopher to accept in setting out his position. Surely a philosopher has the right if not the duty to inquire whether this determining framework which theology assserts can humanly be made sense of.

A more striking case in point is Louis Dupre's *The Other Dimension*.[11] Dupre is not reluctant to take on the meaning of theological doctrines. His book is an impressive attempt to bring Christian doctrines up-to-date by giving them philosophical shape.

There is, however, a curious ambiguity at the base of the whole project and the ambiguity is evident at the end of his chapter on revelation. Up to the last three pages of the chapter the treatment is not much different from traditional theological treatises. At that point the author writes: "One final question of great importance for the development of a religious tradition initiated by a historical revelation is whether such a tradition can envision the possibility of a new beginning." [12] In one long paragraph he then sets out the problem of the concept of an historical revelation and the revolt against the concept today. He further indicates that the issues of community, authority and tradition are all up for grabs in the contemporary religious explosion. But he then ends the chapter with this extraordinary conclusion:

> The philosopher is not qualified to take sides on this issue because the concept of Church is not a logical construction, but a complex, intrinsically religious reality on which he can reflect only *as it exists*. It is precisely the structuring of the religious community which is in full turmoil, even within the established Churches. Since the possibility of revelatory innovation depends on this structure, he must leave the subject to the developing religious reality.[13]

With the asserting of that amazing opinion he buries the main topic of his book. His intention to reflect on what exists is a good one but his last sentence makes the Christian church into a logical construct that takes precedence over "revelatory innovation." Changing church structure is in large part dependent on first changing the meaning of the word revelation. The philosopher is one of the few people who is qualified to "take sides" on who owns the words, how they are to be defined and whether a particular group's meaning makes any sense. Only if one assumes that the current ecclesiastical institution has exclusive right to the basic religious realities would a philosopher sit by waiting to see how the institution will develop. But the assumption that church equals religious reality is what is wrong with the institution to start with. We should not expect much developing if the institution is left to fend for itself.

3

The problem of religious foundations is obscured by the use of the word faith as the basic religious category. Christian philosophers and Christian exegetes seem to agree on one thing, namely, that the religious question is one of faith. Unfortunately, the philosophical enterprise can be completed without even inquiring whether an exegete's faith is compatible with it. The philosopher defers to the theologian on the meaning of Christian faith. From the opposite direction, the exegete can borrow all kinds of insights from modern philosophy while never inquiring whether reliance on an ancient document as one's criterion of truth is compatible with what a philosopher means by faith.

The word faith is incapable of functioning as the basic religious category. If we are to make any progress in understanding religion we need concepts that are relational, social, and institutional from the start. Faith is an important philosophical word that expresses a subjective attitude of openness to and trust in the whole of reality. It is precisely this positive and appropriate sense of the word that is diametrically opposed to "Christian faith" or any religious faith.

Christian theology, almost from the start, recognized some problem with using the word faith. Augustine, Aquinas, Luther and Calvin struggled admirably for the proper emphasis of meaning. Not only has the problem remained but it has gotten considerably worse since the scientific revolution. "To take something on faith" is almost everywhere considered to be a human deficiency except in the Christian church. One cannot easily override the solidly established meaning of the word faith in modern languages. There is a struggle to maintain the positive meaning of faith but that meaning belongs to philosophy and to the human race, not to the Christian church as a religious group.

The negative meaning of faith, that is, a lack of first-hand knowledge with a consequent reliance on someone else's knowledge, is a meaning that occasionally has to function in religion. But I see no reason why that kind of faith should be admired in religion, any more than it is in politics, economics or football. There is no reason why the word faith should show up any more frequently in religion than anywhere else.[14] I have little hope of a total elimination of the word but I do think we could stop calling people "believers" when we mean participants in a religious body and stop referring to "the Christian faith" when we mean Christian scriptures, Christian doctrine, Christian tradition, etc. Otherwise, Christian theologians will never take seriously the magnitude of the problem confronting them. While they say apparently radical things they keep covering over the problem with what is most problematic. They cannot grasp that many people want knowledge, not faith, and these people consider their absence of faith a virtue. What many religiously alive people want is inquiry, discovery, experience, knowledge and symbolism; all of these demands would seem to be legitimate but incapable of being subsumed under faith.

The following passage from Robert Bellah's *Beyond Belief* raises most of the right issues in this area:

> Especially since Kant, there has been increasing realization that . . . the most fundamental cultural forms are neither objective nor subjective, but the very way in which the two are related. . . . This way of thinking allowed the collapse of the traditional certainties without the loss of faith and commitment, an appre-

hension beautifully expressed by Wallace Stevens when he says, "We believe without belief, beyond belief." This shivering of the objective notion of belief allows a reassessment of religion in general and provides a key to why the collapse of belief has not been followed by the end of religion.[15]

The main distinctions which have traditionally been used show up in this passage. The first is found in the Stevens line paradoxically contrasting "to believe" and "belief." A second is the contrast between "faith" and "belief." The third way of trying to get at this issue is to distinguish "believe in" and "believe that." All three of these distinctions are linguistically defensible and they can be helpful within a good, philosophical framework. What they cannot do is establish a "Christian faith."

There is in these distinctions an attempt to bring out a verbal rather than nominal meaning to faith. In the Jewish and Christian scriptures faith was most often an activity of moving, relying upon, trusting, etc. The modern English noun faith cannot capture that sense of movement. The verb "to believe" is therefore introduced but that word is inevitably connected to "belief," a word weaker than faith.

For using the word "believe" a further precision was introduced, the distinction between "believe in" and "believe that." The former phrase is an attempt to avoid reducing "believing" to the holding of beliefs. "To believe in" is not followed by beliefs but by God, the universe, people, etc. By inventing the form "credo in" the Latin church tried to hold on to both the trusting activity and the doctrinal orthodoxy in the same word. It was a great try but the word was too narrow a space in which to work out a religious life. The result was subtleties among theologians, but among "the faithful" there was a reduction of believing to the lowest demand psychologically, educationally and religiously. That is, believing meant accepting what church officials or official texts say is so. Church officials on their part were not and are not notably strong in protesting against this distortion.

The Christian movement at its best was an attempt to carry forward the positive attitude toward the world stemming from Hebraic and Hellenic influences. Christianity's flaw was that it claimed to have the final answer which could already be put into words. The Jew could say "he who believes" and not feel he was omitting anything. "It is not by any means an abbreviated terminus, arising from the permissible omission of 'in God.' Indeed, the addition of this takes from the idea its essential character, or at least weakens it." [16] Believing was for the Jew the stance toward God and the universe.

The Christian church correctly sensed that this attitude of "believing in" is especially reflected in our attitude toward other persons. The category of person grew with this kind of believing. Since Christianity grew up around one person, it seemed that the test was now available for "believing in." Because God was now manifest in a person, belief in that person was belief in God. That sounds logical and it might work well enough if the one called Christ were available as a person to be believed in. But since the first century, the word Christ has no obvious reference to any person on earth. The word refers to documents and doctrines. The Christian church short-circuited "believing in" by adding a noun. Belief in God and belief in Christ were of practical necessity translated into the holding of statements as true that could not be verified for oneself. Church officials have always insisted that faith was not merely that, but if you wished to be a (Christian) believer faith necessarily included that.

The meaning of "believing in" lived on within Christianity and occasionally surfaced in reformers. Unfortunately, they usually staked their reforms on the Christian scriptures, which was not the place to go with this problem. But since the Christian church was interested in beliefs, where was one to go who simply wished to "believe in"? The twentieth century, in the breaking of a Christian hegemony of religious words, now offers an answer: Rediscover the Jewish religious attitude, appreciate tribal religion and enter into dialogue with the East.

All of this religious search has to take place in the context of the modern world. The positive meaning of "believing in" which was submerged in Christianity re-emerged as one of the premises of the Western scientific and technological world. The church, not recognizing the child of its own bearing, has often attacked as irreligious those who trust in the world, but those people are the heirs of the "believing in" attitude cultivated if not invented by Jewish and Christian religions. The following passage from Teilhard de Chardin would scandalize many church people but it flows directly from that attitude:

> If, as the result of some interior revolution, I were to lose in succession my faith in Christ, my faith in a personal God, and my faith in spirit, I feel that I should continue to *believe* invincibly *in the world*. The world (its value, its infallibility and its goodness) —that, when all is said and done, is the first, the last, and the only thing in which I believe. It is by this faith that I live. And it is to this faith, I feel, that at the moment of death, rising above all doubts, I shall surrender myself.[17]

There is nothing pollyannaish about this attitude as if one could romantically put aside all the harshness, suffering and seeming absurdity of the world. Teilhard "be-

lieves in" the world because there is nothing else to believe in and ultimately one either trusts in it or one doesn't.
To choose "the Christian faith" is not to affirm the only
world there is, and it is in this way that Christian faith
unwittingly aligns itself with modern nihilism. "A ni-
hilist," Albert Camus once wrote, "is not one who believes
in nothing but rather one who does not believe in what
exists." All faiths, that is, all elaborated systems of belief,
stand opposed to believing in what exists. "Believing in"
is the attitude which can link men and women everywhere, it is an attitude indispensable to human survival.
If faith is to function positively in a religious body it
must be firmly situated as a human prerogative of the religious body and not be allowed to float out into the sphere
of objects so as to become the possession of some particular group.

4

The inadequacy of the word faith is reflected in what
is supposed to be a radical new approach to Christian theology. Liberation is the word which is to unlock everything and the church's faith is to be the liberator. Harvey
Cox, calling for a revolution in theological method, writes:
"If the liberation of humankind is seen as the *purpose* of
Christianity, and if theology is to serve the purpose of the
faith, then theology too must be directed toward human
liberation." [18] This is the kind of clarion call for action
which is difficult to oppose but some skepticism might still
be in order. The proposed change is not a novelty at all.
Christianity has only been too eagerly ready to liberate
everybody. Christian theology, instead of restraining the
tendency, has been too willing to be the mouthpiece of the
officials ("to serve the purposes of the faith"). There is

an utter absence of epistemological critique locked into that use of "the faith." One presumes that the church has the faith and the big question is how to direct it at other people. The illusion of assuming that Christianity has the world's truth in its possession can be protected by directing the church outward to be the "servant" of the world.

The call for a "servant church" in much theological writing should make one suspicious. One would think that we should be trying to eliminate servants altogether. Anyone who glories today in being a servant is possibly sick or else he has something up his sleeve. In this case the servant claims to have nothing—except the key to the universe. The Christian church in the past made all kinds of claims to superiority of virtue and assurance of salvation. Under the pressure of external criticism and indubitable fact the claims have been slowly whittled down.

The giving up of ground must be carefully examined, however, because the one thing which was retained is the superior knowledge. "The Christian is he who already knows." [19] A church that becomes a superpsychoanalyst of the world is less tractable and more dangerous. The retention of "the faith" as the secret key to the world's problems is an exacerbation, not an amelioration, of the church's arrogance. The opposite direction would have been preferable, that is, to claim that the Christian church should manifest all kinds of distinctive qualities but that the one way it should not claim to be different is in knowing more than any other body.

What is widely assumed today to be the most radical Christian theology is painfully embedded in the most inadequate categories of the Christian past. The words are interconnected: *The church has a faith* which *she preaches to liberate mankind.* Only the word "which" is not a problem in this sentence. All of the words on social action which get added do not change the theological assumption at work. The questions which beg to be asked are: Who liberates the liberators from their illusion of having the faith? Who liberates the people who are in the church from the oppressiveness of officials and preaching?

An interesting litmus test in Christian theology is the use of the word man. Liberation is almost always for "man" or "mankind." The abstract masculine pronoun is nearly always correlated to the absence of epistemological criticism about "the faith." This use of the word man is joined with an insensitivity to the enslavement which Christianity can cause. Seventeenth century science was also going to liberate "man" by giving "him" power over nature. Unfortunately, as many writers point out today, it was not "man" that existed but individual men who had power over other men and women.[20] Injecting more technical power into that arrangement did not free "man" from nature. Some men became even more powerful but most men and most women became less powerful. In addition, the overall rhetoric generated an irreverent attitude toward our nonhuman friends in nature.

Instead of pronouncing on the "liberation of man" Christian theologians might better be concerned with the liberation of some men from other men, the liberation of women in the church, and the liberation of the nonhuman world from the domination of "man." The concern would best be shown by theology purifying itself and the church of oppressive language. Christian theology in its faddish aspects makes pronouncements on the ecological and feminist movements. But when it is at its more serious business Christian theology exposes its antiecological and sexist bias by its endless talk of "man." The problem will not be resolved by sticking in a few "humankinds" for "mankind" but by changing the method of how religious writing is done, by whom it is written and in what situations it originates.

A striking example of the general pattern I have been describing is Gustavo Gutierrez's *Theology of Liberation*.[21] The book was hailed as a major step forward in Christian writing. To the extent that it relies on its native South American locale the book is a valuable source of material. Unfortunately, its theological framework is the same kind of thing that has been in European seminaries for decades or centuries. The symptom of what is wrong is the absence of any reference in 323 pages of writing to the fact that his own writing needs liberation from the domination of abstract masculine pronouns. There is probably no language available for avoiding the problem (and translations can worsen it) but it is evident when a writer is struggling against the limits of her or his language.

The church, says Gutierrez, must preach spiritual poverty because "only in this way will the Church be able to fulfill authentically—and with any possibility of being listened to—its prophetic function of denouncing every injustice to man. Only in this way will it be able to preach the word which liberates, the word of genuine brotherhood." [22] Perhaps it is precisely because the church has "preached the word which liberates" that it has created abstractions like brotherhood instead of being part of a world of sisters, brothers, and nonhumans.

My criticism is not particularly directed at Gutierrez. His language is only too typical of Christian writing. If a bishop writes a book it is possible that it have a daring title like *Body Theology*.[23] In the subtitle, however, we have *God's Presence in Man's World*. The contents live up to the subtitle in that the book indeed discusses "man's world." One could hardly guess that the larger part of the Christian church is women and that one of the major problems which the world faces is the illusion of it being a "man's world."

5

There are some attempts among Christian writers to find a base that would be broader than faith. The most promising category in the American language is probably the word experience. There is, in fact, a great deal of writing about experience these days. Very often, however, experience is simply used to serve the purpose of "the faith." Unless the finality of the word faith is challenged, then attempts to relate faith and experience are caught in a bind. When the traditional Christian terminology is maintained, experience has a very restricted meaning, taken to be the first step in a sequence or as a momentary happening.[24]

The word experience does have its difficulties. Both in popular speech and in post-Kantian European philosophy experience is often contrasted to reason, to authority and to history. That meaning would be utterly inadequate for founding philosophical or religious thought. In the United States there is possible a stronger meaning for the word. Experience can have political, social and historical meaning. A use of the word as basic to religion requires fighting against its trivalization, but that is the case with any basic word. Its two advantages are: (1) It has not been co-opted by Christianity. (2) It is capable of bearing personal, bodily, social, political and institutional meaning.

The danger of relying upon experience has always been that one small group in the world dictated what experience should mean for everyone else. We have never been able to consider what "human experience" means because we have had the white or male or Western or Northern or

rich people's version of experience. The frustrating fact
is that we can come to grasp the human meaning of experience only as political institutions are made adequate
for their job. So long as our institutions fail to bring out
the unique experience of each individual and every group
then we are dealing with pale and limited versions of human experience.

The age-old problem of experience being limited and
controlled is still with us today. However, many of the
ancient segregations are at least being challenged today.
The religious movement is at the center of the challenge
in that "religious experience" is the refusal to cut off
experience at the level of the ordinary and established.

The drive to open up experience today has been described by R. D. Laing as blasting our way through fifty
feet of concrete. We have to do it, Laing writes, even at
the risk of chaos, madness and death; from this side of the
wall that is the risk—with no assurances, no guarantees.
True sanity, he goes on to say, would entail the dissolu-
tion of a false ego and the reestablishment of a new ego in
touch with the divine.[25] Laing and many others writing
on this subject today do not have to import religion into
experience or find some bizarre aspect that can be called
a "religious experience." The religious question emerges
as one penetrates all the depths of experience and discovers what is there. If one begins with experience one is
never faced with making a jump from "man" to God.
Rather, it is a question of exploring the endless mysteries
of the human and not-human meanings of experience.
There is no upper limit set upon the word God but there
is likely to be a reticence about God while searching for
an experiential meaning of divine.

The hesitancy of Christianity to embrace experience
is probably well founded. Christian theology would get

more than it had bargained for. In the most comprehensive meaning of experience one does not so much embrace experience as be embraced by it.

In summary, I have been articulating two meanings for the word experience. The second meaning is preferable because it subsumes the best elements of the first while the reverse is not true. Although the first meaning cannot be eliminated, the test of its validity is in the context of the second meaning. In the first meaning: "I have an experience." In the second meaning: "We are engaged in, with, through experience." In the first, experience refers to discrete elements that an individual can possess; in the second, experience is the total matrix of relationships that constitute the world. In the first, experience breaks sharply into rational and irrational elements with the criteria of truth being clarity and intensity; in the second, experience is a field of distinct but related elements and the criterion is integrity. In the first, experience may be opposed by reason, authority or the past; in the second, the opposite of experience is nothing or anything less than wholeness.

My intention has been to describe these two functioning meanings of the word experience. There is no question of one right meaning and one wrong meaning. Both meanings operate, and though the second is more comprehensive, the first obviously has a legitimacy to it. In practice the second has a tendency to reduce to the first, a movement which is encouraged by elitist control groups. Although the reductionist tendency is inevitable I am suggesting that the role of religion is to resist the reduction of experience. In the first meaning of experience there is likely to be much talk of experiences of God. But once the word God is linguistically situated as direct object of experience then the word is reduced to referring to one object among many. In the second meaning, one cannot experience God because God is not a "content" of an experience. But there is more to experience than *what* is experienced. Words like sacred, divine and holy are not experientially meaningless but the meaning is evoked in the midst of prayer, symbolic gesture, metaphor and life/death confrontations. Religious searchers with this meaning of experience are liable to be called atheists by those who have a clear definition of God.

I use the word revelation as practically coextensive with experience. The advantage of the word revelation is that it carries some connotations that the word experience lacks. In addition, I am setting up a direct confrontation between Christian premises and human experience. The word revelation has a specific history within Christianity so that equating the word to experience forces a basic rethinking of the area. Although often hidden under "the faith," the concept of revelation is the linchpin of Christian theology. Either the concept has to be rehabilitated or else eliminated.

The chances of salvaging the word revelation may not seem very great. Nevertheless, despite its checkered history within Christianity, the word still carries interesting overtones. With the renewed interest in magic and madness, miracle and mysticism, mystery and dream, the word revelation may yet come into its own as the appropriate word for our era. Certainly, if the word is to function meaningfully in a religious context it would have to be shown that revelation is a helpful word to describe movies, mental health, politics, sex, ecology, drugs and much else in life. I look for the restoration of the word less from Christian theologians than from science fiction writers and writers on the "paranormal."

I take the word revelation as a possibility for describing the total field of subject-object, organism-environment, human-nonhuman relationships. The word carries within

itself the sense of interrelationship, the personal, the surprising, the enlightening, the sexual. In choosing a word
that does have a specific Christian meaning I cannot be
certain of avoiding all trace of imperialism. My defense
is that the word chosen is a dialogical word that will locate the biases of Christianity as it is filled out in ways
that Christianity does not dictate.

6

The scope of the meaning of revelation can be seen in an
evolutionary scheme of religious development. The possible meaning of revelation corresponds to differences in
the form of religion. Before proposing such a pattern of
development some preliminary comments are necessary
about evolutionary schema and assumptions about time.

The test of my scheme is whether it helps us to speak
comprehensively and consistently about the phenomenon
of religion. The pattern does not imply an ideology imposed on the thing at issue. Even less is the pattern a prediction of things to come. The description is of what is
available in our experience. Perhaps the only dramatic
claim implicit in it is that it does suppose that we are
going through a climactic change in human life.

My pattern has three parts. It would be possible to sub-
divide and have five, six, or more stages.[26] For a reason
which I hope will be quickly evident, I restrict it to three.
Most people who do suggest evolutionary patterns have
three stages and to this extent they seem to agree with
one another. The apparent agreement hides the basic
disagreement on whether the development is a straight line
of continuous progress or whether the previous stages are
incorporated into subsequent ones.

My stages are somewhat misleading if called one, two

and three. They might be better called *A, A′* and *B*. The implication is that *A* and *A′* exist in some tension, if not outright conflict. Furthermore, *B* emerges not by leaving behind the others but by some kind of interaction of the two. This does not presume a perfect, logical, Hegelian synthesis but simply an interplay of elements from the past as the material of our present. Differently stated, I do not presume that human progress comes about by shucking off the past but by rediscovering in new form elements we thought we had left behind us. In this regard the choice of category to bear an evolutionary process is crucial. If the category is not relational and social then a human evolution is impossible.

An instructive example here is the idea of consciousness. It is common today to talk of progress in relation to consciousness. Christian writers regularly use consciousness in conjunction with faith. The trouble with both consciousness and faith is that they are individualistic—faith in its positive meaning of an inner, subjective attitude of openness, and consciousness in its clear reference to an individual's awareness. At some point faith and consciousness can go beyond the individual but only into the mystical. They do not operate well as communal or institutional descriptions. There is only so much one can do with the idea of consciousness and that is not sufficient for describing human and religious evolution.

A famous book of a few years ago, *The Greening of America,* tried to describe the United States with the terms consciousness I, II, III.[27] The book was severely criticized in almost all quarters. Much of the criticism seemed to be peripheral to the main issues and some of it was quite inaccurate. The author was widely criticized for a simplistic theory of straight-line progress and the presumption that the past is bad, the present is good, the future is better. In many ways he did seem to be pushing that his stage II was better than I and that III was better than I and II. There are, however, some apparent anomalies. The three stages are not the history of the country; stage I is indicated to have begun in mid-nineteenth century. Furthermore, it was often noted but seldom analyzed that stages I and II often blur into each other.

Actually, there are three stages in the book but they are not consciousness I, II and III. There are instead: (1) a true consciousness which preceded I; (2) a false consciousness of I, II; (3) a return to true consciousness in III. Far from glorifying the present and expecting that the future will be better, he is pessimistic about most of all that. There is no straight line of progress because he is directing attention to the distant (U.S.) past when life could be lived in pristine purity. Underneath a straight line there almost always lurks a circle.[28]

The reaction that the book received was more interesting than the book itself.[29] It was greeted with exaggerated praise, then savagely attacked and then quickly forgotten. A fair judgment on the book may not yet be possible, but eventually the book may come to be seen as an interesting work which had the virtue of shaking up established orthodoxies but failed to create a workable scheme for understanding the youth movement of the sixties.[30]

My interest in this failure concerns the fact that the project was doomed by the choice of consciousness as the main category. Consciousness is not a workable concept for discussing evolution, whether it be political, social or religious. It is tempting to use consciousness because it seems clear that consciousness does expand, grow or heighten. Also, we seem with consciousness to know what we are talking about: the specific power that constitutes each individual and which when combined through many individuals constitutes the history of an era. But Freud and Jung, if not Marx, should have taught us that individuals and the world do not progress by one-dimensional addition to the light and content of consciousness. The nub of the problem is the relation of conscious and not-conscious. A theoretical scheme which relies on consciousness cannot even recognize that problem. As a result, the increase in consciousness may lead to exhaustion before a world that can be seen as complex but cannot be righted by consciousness. Not having a way to alter contemporary structures, consciousness is likely to turn nostalgically to the past.

7

As the above example indicates, every evolutionary theory implies a theory of time. I would like to try to make explicit the meaning of time that I presuppose. My contrast of two meanings of time parallels what I have already said of two meanings of experience.

The first conception of time can be called mechanical/artificial; the second can be described as personal/organismic. As with experience, the second can subsume the first but not vice versa. In the first, time is conceived of as a series of points and is usually diagrammed with the present at the center, the past to the left and the future to the right. This conception of time is so utterly pervasive in Western, technological society that it is difficult to become aware that this meaning of time was largely an invention and not at all obvious to most people.

Aristotle had defined time as the measure of motion conceived as before and after. Modern science found this definition perfectly acceptable (at least until Einstein) and for the purpose of measuring time invented the clock. It may be amusing to see that earlier centuries were so fascinated by the clock, but it is doubtful that we have ever recovered from the fascination. The clock seems to be the chief model for thinking about life. In the midst of every heated discussion there usually comes that time when someone proposes to swing the pendulum back toward the center. The solution is usually a bad restatement of the problem providing what seems to be the obvious answer except that it mistakes people for clocks.

The significance of this meaning of time can hardly be exaggerated. What a group thinks of life as a whole is embodied in its sense of time. Norman O. Brown notes that we are now aware that the Hopi sense of time is directly related to their religious values. But, Brown continues, "the essential point is to see that the classical Western sense of time, Newtonian time, was a religion, which, like all religions, was taken by its adherents (both the physicists and the economists) to be absolute objective truth. Once again we see that 'secular rationalism' is really a religion." [31] For several centuries the best that Christian theology seemed able to say of God was that "he" is a great watchmaker. One can sympathize with Voltaire who expressed little enthusiasm for a God who makes clocks.

There is obviously some truth to the notion of time as a series of measurable points. Certainly, there is an obvious productiveness to this notion of time. Modern technology is unthinkable without the clock mentality. Nonetheless, if this mechanical/artificial conception is the exclusive or primary model of time, then there will be violence to human and nonhuman life. Where is the substance to any life if the past is no longer with us, the future has not arrived and the present is a fleeting moment?

There is another meaning of time which does not begin with fleeting moments. I have called this personal/organismic time. Here the word present means to live relationally, to be present is to be in the presence of. There is no play upon words here. Present taken to be a point in sequence (or a point in space) is an element abstracted from a relationship. The primary meaning of present is the relation of man and man, woman and woman, woman and man, human and nonhuman.

The main choice which the woman or man has is the choice either to live profoundly in the present or to live superficially in the present. To live superficially is not really to be there in the only place one can be. If one lives profoundly in the present one discovers the past as the gift of previous generations that forms the substance of our lives. One also discovers the future as the real though limited possibilities of our presence to one another. The opposite of present is neither past nor future; the opposite of present is absent. I deny that one can overemphasize the present (though one can misconceive it); the present is all there is and all there ever will be as presence changes.

I would reject the stated or unstated premise of Christian theology today that primitive religions were interested in the past and a sophisticated religion (Christianity) ought to be mainly concerned about the future. I view with alarm the coalition of theologians and futurologists who with Russian and U.S. bulldozers wish to save the benighted pagans from their past.

Religious people in the primitive world did not live in the past. They lived in the present, caring for the things of this world and worshipping its gods. I would think that anyone who claims to be religious would resist that obsession with the future which often typifies the United States. No one who grew up with the slogan "progress is our most important product" has to be told about striving for the future. There is a sickness of "purposefulness," as John Maynard Keynes called it, "an overstrained goal consciousness." [32] Christian theology's infatuation with the future supports some of the most exploitative aspects of U.S. advertising and technology.

The primitive religious mentality which was concerned with the present did have an inadequate notion of time. In much of African religion, for example, there is no future or the future is simply immediate consequences. Movement is more toward the past than a future. The African tribe was in touch with their ancestors. The longer a person lived the closer he or she approached those ancestors. At death a person finally reached the past. This conception of time may seem to us silly or preposterous. Undoubtedly it is an inadequate conception but one that may not be more inadequate than our own.[33]

The West, I have said, practically invented the future; that is, our ancestors discovered that there were far more possibilities in the present than primitive peoples had imagined. The discovery was confined to certain Western countries but is now spreading rapidly to other places (including African cities). The discovery of the future could be progress as long as it is not ripped from its context in the present.

That Western technology could be a (limited) help to primitively developed countries is a thesis grasped with ease. What is still inconceivable to many people is that we may have much to learn from African tribes or North American natives. It is not so much a question of going backward (the serial notion of time) as going down (to the past), in (to ourselves) and outward (to other peoples). This description is not primitivism or romanticism but simply a refusal to accept a flattened out version of life, a version that always promises a better future. The attitude is caught in a poignant line of Beckett's *Endgame*: "Do you believe in the life to come?" asks Clov; Hamm answers: "Mine was always that." [34]

The choice is between a present which integrates past

and future, or a past and future split apart in a neglected present. Christian theology's attempt to find a future by exegeting past texts is still a refusal to be present. Christian theology may correctly sense that if it did deal with the present it would cease to control its world and have to become something radically different. So long as Christian theology stays with futurology it is in no danger of facing up to its own methodological problems. The future is the final piece of that ideology which concerns church-preaching-faith-liberation-man. Instead of talking endlessly about the liberation of "man" in the future, a religious body would be a place for men, women and nonhumans to experience in the present.

8

It remains now to place these elements into a threefold scheme of experience and revelation for understanding religious development. In briefest fashion, the three stages can be described this way: (1) The experience is of *man confronted* by a divine *power*. (2) The belief is that *men possess* a divine *message* with which to interpret experience. (3) The experience is of communities of *men and women dis-covering* the divine in *relationships*. If one were to use the word revelation as the basic religious category in this scheme, the meaning of revelation would be different in each of the three stages. In the first, revelation is a nonrational force; in the second, revelation refers to a rational thing perhaps deposited in written statements; in the third, revelation is a relation in which the human participates.

The nouns in the three stages should be noticed: man, men, communities of men/women. The first two nouns are not a slip into male chauvinism but an accurate description of who is doing the controlling. In the first it is man or collective and tribal man who is the recipient of religious activity. Even in matriarchies man seems to be the right word. In the second, the term men seems to be the exact one for the emergence of the individual, that is, individualized, rationalized, bureaucratic men. In the third, there are communities which include men and women in a form that combines the tribal and the individual.

The verbs are intended to correlate to the nouns: (1) Confronted means to be met and seized by some force not under one's control. (2) Possess refers to what is under individual and rational control. (3) Discover is a word intended to catch both activity and receptivity; one must work actively even while aware that truth and life are unveiled in receptivity to others.

This threefold pattern is a general typology which is intended as an instrument of understanding. If it is useful then the life of an individual and the life of the race ought to be reflected to some degree in it. Not every bit of data needs to be forced into it nor can exact chronological lines be drawn for it. What is suggested by it is that progress is not a straight line of development but that the third stage emerges from some synthesizing of the previous two. Although three is not a rejection of two, there is no smooth continuity of development from two to three. The third stage is not a prediction of what will happen but something that has happened on a small scale and may now be happening on a larger scale. The scheme makes no predictions about the outcome of history but it does give us signs to watch: the relation of person to group, the relation of humans to nonhumans and the relation of individual quest for unity to a world not under the control of individuals.

As an interpretive scheme for the individual it suggests

that adulthood is signified by the reappropriation of the childhood we sought to forget in adolescence. On the larger cloth of history the pattern locates the rise of a form of religion in the past and the crisis today. It should be evident why there is no four, five or six in this model. Stage three is not third in one sequence but a mode of relation always being reached to some degree. Individualization is not exclusively a modern phenomenon; ancient people could be quite individualistic. Nevertheless, there still seems to be an unparalleled step in the religious movements of 1,500 to 3,000 years ago, as well as in the religious crisis around us in this century.

9

Some further comments are needed regarding the details of experience in each of these religious stages. For "man" of the first stage the earth is alive and full of gods, both male and female. Religions are called naturistic if directed mainly to the great cosmic forces which cover the earth (rocks, plants, wind, stars, sky). They are animistic if peopled by spiritual beings such as spirits, souls, genii, demons. Most people have elements of both naturism and animism. The god of these phenomena could be reached through a tribal totem and by repetition of archetypal actions.

It is inaccurate to call primitive religious worship idolatry or the worship of creatures. What Evans-Pritchard writes of the African tribe he studied would be more generally true:

> It would be quite contrary to Nuer thought . . . and it would even be absurd to them to say that sky, moon, rain and so forth are in themselves, simply or collec-

tively, God. God is Spirit, which, like wind and air, is invisible and ubiquitous. But though God is not one of these things he is in them in the sense that he reveals himself through them. In this sense . . . he is in the sky, falls in the rain, shines in the sun and moon, and blows in the wind.[35]

Religion was a coming to terms with the controlling powers of the universe. There was a natural basis for being a contemplative. Not being in a position to push and pull nature to human purposes, the primitive had to achieve some kind of harmony. The religious reaction to the great powers of the world was worship. Religious rites provided the necessary stabilization of life at its most critical moments: birth, initiation, marriage, harvest, war, death. "The believer who has communicated with his god is not merely a man who sees new truths of which the unbeliever is ignorant; he is a man who is *stronger*. He feels within him more force, either to endure the trials of existence, or to conquer them." [36]

Strength was needed to endure suffering but ancient religion was not all terror and anxiety. Life was celebrated in the present and there was a kinship with the earth and its other inhabitants. Although man was weak he could share in the life of the gods. Shamanistic religion assumed that at least on occasion man can rise to the level of the gods. There was at least a center to life to which one could turn and there was a path for patiently pursuing life.[37]

The modern world was going to get rid of all that magic and mystery through rational explanations and technical means. But it is those forces which have come back to haunt us. In the middle of sophisticated suburbs and technological metropolises, the irrational has surfaced again, often in bizarre form. The ocean, trees and earth are now demanding that "man" listen. There seems to be no more

future without a recovery of some of the attitudes that typi-
fied primitive life: reverence, sensitivity, receptivity, wonder, awe and delight. The recovery is not one that is all
sweetness and light. There is also terror buried deep in
the modern psyche where it has been inaccessible to ritual.
The progress of a third stage requires our recognition that
we are more like "primitive man" than we like to think.
The first and third stages bear remarkable similarities.

10

The second stage of religious development is the one in
which the Christian church comfortably settled. Here religion refers to membership in an institution administered
by men. Revelation within this context means that a message from God has been bequeathed to these men. The
men who run the institution are usually intelligent, or at
least highly rational; they are conscientious, especially
of other peoples' consciences; they are highly dedicated—
in fact, they work a little too hard. What they are in danger of forgetting is the dictum of Martin Buber's that "no
one is so possessed as he who thinks that he possesses
God." Men poring over their books in library, office and
pulpit can do nothing except reenforce the inadequate
idea of revelation that is assumed here. So long as Christian theology is written almost exclusively by clergymen
it will continue to shore up the inadequate religious imagery that is theology's problem.

The role of the clergyman has been to read the Christian books and then tell these truths to the people. The
nature of the church officials' work was consequent upon
the existence of a "Christian revelation" while the clergyman's control of theology further supported the notion of
revelation as truths which God has supplied to Christi-

anity. No talk of event, encounter or spirit has in the least shaken the functioning meaning of revelation: somewhere there is something which the Christian church has which deserves to be called revelation.

The crisis of Christianity is very much a crisis of a male god. The problem is not dealt with in a nervous parenthesis saying: Sorry about that, girls.[38] A god who directs everything toward the "liberation of man in the future" is obviously a he. A god experienced in the presence of a community rooted to the earth will have qualities that are masculine and feminine, personal and impersonal, monotheistic and polytheistic. The Christian movement at its origins might have captured this multi-image approach to the ultimate power of the universe; but the rich mystery was quickly reduced.

The Christian church has for many centuries been burdened with an inadequate image of the relation of divine and human. Revelation became the orders which an all powerful father gives to his disobedient sons. The main job in such an organization is to tell people what the truth is and set up controls to help them do the truth. Theologians came to refer to the "revealed word" (the book where it is contained). Eventually, Christianity came to speak of revealed religion (in the seventeenth century) when the entire system had become divinized.

The unspoken model of the religious life is the work of the preacher. God revealing himself is approximately equivalent to a clergyman giving a sermon. Religious writing might not be better but it would certainly be different if it originated with airline stewardesses, longshoremen, mental patients, sanitationmen, schoolchildren, elevator operators, etc. If I were asked to suggest some images for founding the religious life it would never occur to me to use preaching or messages. What would come to my mind might be: an old woman placing flowers on her husband's grave, a man seated on a mountain overlooking a city, a neighborhood political meeting, two adolescents falling in love, group theory, a psychotherapist with her client, or a hundred other images that have personal, communal, social, political, mystical, ecological aspects. It must be admitted, however, that the Christian notion of revelation is consistent with the Christian church's form. A group which thinks it has from God a message for everyone else should look very much like the Christian church looks.

11

The last sentence indicates why, despite the efforts of theologians and pastors, the concept of revelation has changed so little in Christianity. What would be needed is a change in institutional form. The movement from a second to a third stage of development would require a change in the relation of men and men, men and women, women and women.

The third stage of religious development is one in which the full range of human experience would finally be available. The phrase "community of men and women" is redundant since any use of the word community, unless otherwise specified, includes men and women. Community includes more diversity than men and women but that one needs special emphasis. The description of an integrated religious body is the task of the following chapters. At this point, however, a few principles should be clear:

1. A religious body would have to provide for the full emergence of individual personality and at the same time be an experience of the tribal, collective or communal character of the race.

a) As part of this principle a religious body would

have to provide for ego loss, that is, for a person going out of his or her mind without being destroyed. What follows the loss of a narrow egocentric world is not agreed upon in the religious traditions.

b) Another part of this principle is that a religious body would be a place for contemplative prayer rhythmically related to intense social action.[39] Neither the mystical searchings of a spiritual elite nor the simple devotional life of the people should be excluded, either in principle or in fact.

2. A religious body has to live from its own roots and traditions. It must have the concreteness and particularity of an old human reality. It must also have come to terms with its past so that without apology or defensiveness it can enter into exchange with other religious and non-religious groups. Devotion to one's tradition, people and activity is not at all incompatible with tolerance for others.

3. A religious body today would have to reestablish kinship with the earth and at the same time not cease to be part of a technologically developing world. It would resist the futuristic obsession built into the technologically planned world but it would not do so by attempting to retreat into a nostalgic past. It would reject Christian theology's choice of time over space. A religious body is a people who love both their place and time. The feel for the contours of the earth and the love for one's home are part of any religious people's experience.

These principles are merely that. They do not represent a solution but they do represent some progress in understanding. They suggest that some reforms currently being advocated within the Christian church are counterproductive. They also suggest that some of the antichurch movement is also not going in the right direction. Only by carefully working out what seem to be irreconcilable opposites can a religious body be understood.

Chapter Four

Community as Religious

Community is one of the two bases on which I am re-defining the meaning of religious body. The project may seem negated by the fact that the word community itself has no agreed-upon definition. But this fact is simply an unavoidable difficulty when dealing with the most profound of human realities. Only a word that is ambiguous in meaning and rich in association can function as the encompassing term for describing the human.

Ambiguity is not the same as confusion. A word can possess distinct shades of meaning and various levels of tone while still having an exact definition. For such a rich word, it is imperative to set some limits on its usage so that its wealth is not dissipated in overuse and misuse. As I have indicated already, the vague or parasitical use of basic human terms is one way in which language and human beings are systematically destroyed. Individuals or industries bent on exploitation can acquire a veil of legitimacy by hooking on to nice-sounding words like community.

The task, therefore, is to fix a meaning which is both comprehensive and consistent. By comprehensive I mean that it covers all the obvious data and possibly even reveals

more data than we had suspected. By consistent I mean
that there is some kind of inner logic in its variety of applications. The logic does not have to be inductive or de-
ductive but there has to be a minimum compatibility of
metaphors. The overextension of the word community
evacuates the word of any consistent meaning to the point
where it can become an empty filler in sentences. Conversely, the overcontrol of the word to the point where it
would only mean, for example, a section of a city or town,
would eliminate the effectiveness of the term as a comprehensive description of the human.

The use of the term community here is not sociological
though I am trying not to neglect what sociology has done
with the word in the last one hundred years. The use here
might be called philosophical while at the same time
there is an appropriation of psychological and sociological
material. The concept of community long antedates the
empirical social sciences, but these sciences have concre-
tized, corrected and added to ancient and premodern notions of community. My definition of community also has
reference to religion both because of my purpose and because the philosophical and religious history of the word
is intertwined. However, most of this discussion of community will proceed without explicit reference to religion.
Only after the main description of community do I raise
the possibility of placing the adjective religious before it.

The first thing to be said about the word is that it refers to human unity. There are many kinds of union, unity
and unification but community is used in reference to
something specifically human. That fact raises some puzzling questions about what specifically differentiates the
human from the nonhuman. It also raises the need to have
other words which contrast to community when describing nonhuman unities. Such unities would be those in
which: (1) the uniting elements are not human; (2) the

elements are human but they do not unite in the way appropriate to humans.

Each of these contrasting cases has its own debatable areas. In the first case, any unity that is recognized and named by the human does not entirely exclude the human. The word community may therefore have greater extension than might first be assumed. For example, a dog kennel would not usually be called a community but I would not wish prematurely to exclude all animal participation in this definition. In the second case, the word "appropriate" in the above description of human relationships needs unraveling before we can decide where to set a limit on the word. For example, an assassin and his or her victim will not fall under the definition of community. Also, a federal prison is a form of unity that lacks the characteristics I ascribe to community. However, there is a continuum of form from those that are more destructive to those that are questionable as forms of human union. Humans can transcend the deficiencies of form, and community can spring up in the most unlikely places.

What is already apparent in the discussion is that the word community is not neutral in value. The word community carries overtones of desirability and positive value. A human unity means at the least that the human is not destroyed but that it is in some (perhaps unexpected) ways affirmed. In short, the word community always has a moral sense to it, a fact that should hardly be surprising in that moral originally means the way humans act.

The question of morality is unavoidable in examining the question of human unity. The attempt to be antiseptically amoral on the question of community almost surely leads to immorality, that is, actions against the human. The following passage from Robert Nisbet should not be surprising and should perhaps be read as a warning:

Community begins as a moral value; only gradually does the secularization of this concept become apparent in sociological thought in the century. Precisely the same is true of alienation, authority, status, and the others. The moral texture of these ideas is never wholly lost. Even in the scientific writing of Weber and Durkheim, a full century after these ideas had made their first appearance, the moral element remains vivid. The great sociologists never ceased to be moral philosophers.[1]

If the word community carries this moral value it would be a suitable word to describe the ultimate human ideal. Community would be the most appropriate, most affirmative, most encompassing ideal. There seems to be nothing inherently reductive or pejorative in the word to prevent its use in that way. In addition, there seem to be few competing words for expressing the hope and the ideal of the human race.

There is one problem that does arise if we choose to make community the truly human unity. When one begins pushing in that direction there is no apparent place to stop or to rest in reality. Every existing unity is exposed as deficient because it is obviously not the unity of the human. A community would obviously have to include more than one country or one race. But even all the people living in the world are not the unity of the human.

There is a logical attractiveness in skipping over all these deficiencies in search of "humanity." Philosophy has often gone in that direction. However, logic itself can be destructive of the human so that, paradoxically, a relentless pursual of the definition of human unity can eliminate the concreteness of human beings.[2] Logic itself has to be put in question with the search for community. A restraint upon the philosophical mind has to be exercised by the data of empirical sciences and the particularity of religious tradition. An adequate "definition" of human unity would require the invention of a new kind of "logic" which does not abstract to reach unity. Community, used to designate a unity that includes human differences, is a safeguard against eliminating individual humans for the sake of collective humanity.

In attempting to cope with the problem raised in the preceding paragraph, I wish to propose a two-pronged meaning for the word community. First, there is the idea and ideal of human unity which has not been realized but which is at issue in philosophical and religious quest. Second, there is the realization of that ideal in microcosmic form; the realization is never perfectly achieved but it can be reached at a high enough degree to merit appropriation of the term community. The two uses are part of a single relation; the existing community by embodying the ideal demonstrates that it is possible not only in thought but in practice. The two are also connected in practice by innumerable intermediary structures. These political, economic and other kinds of structures would best be called something other than communities. Their purpose is to be the connecting link between the actual, existing community and the ideal community yet to be realized. Some further comment is needed here about the ideal unity. I will then proceed to discuss both the intermediary association and the small actuality. After that I return once more to the dream of ultimate unity.

Unity implies that there are diverse elements which need unifying. The fact of manyness is obvious enough. One way to resolve the problem of "the one and the many" is to eliminate the many or at least deny ultimate significance to the apparent diversity of the world. This tendency is a strong one, perhaps the main one in the history of philosophy and religion. One reason for approaching religion through the question of community is to resist this tendency. Implicit in my approach is a criticism of religious traditions which move in the direction of eliminating diversity. Every difference is not necessarily good but neither can it be assumed that all differences must be eliminated for the sake of unity.

What is claimed here is that community, understood as both ideal and actual, may hold the key to religious matters. In turn, religious symbolism together with the modern sciences may be able to fill out the meaning of community in a way that would improve on ancient philosophy.

The human, individually and collectively, is directed toward unification with what is beyond. The first and continuing experience of humanness is to be confronted with otherness. The other is a threat to the security of human existence but it is also the environment which makes survival and growth possible. There is, of course, an ambiguity in referring to what is "other than the human" because what an individual human being experiences as other includes other humans. This intrahuman otherness is what has slowly emerged into philosophical prominence and now urgently calls our attention. It is part of the problem but also a possible key to the "one and the many." In raising the question of unity as human unity I am interested in a drive toward unity that does not eliminate the human in the achievement of oneness.

If it is objected that this approach is a narcissistic, egoistic and selfish way to raise the question of one and many, I am willing to admit that that may be the case. Nonetheless, as a human I think it is the proper way for humans to ask the question. I think it could even be claimed that humans cannot raise the question without overtly or covertly making it the question of the kind of human unity. I choose to ask about human unity as openly and explicitly as possible. One must be very careful about proposing non-duality as the highest religious ideal.[3] In some places today, it is suggested that the choice is between individualism and a united world. Individualism is then attacked in the name of a vague, undifferentiated whole. However, individualistic and collectivistic go together. The alternative to them is a universe which supports the personal and communal.

2

The great ideal obviously does not exist in actuality but what we do have are small demonstration projects. For reasons which may be clear already, the chief quality of community is mutuality of relationship. There are other qualities which can describe community but they follow upon the specifically human activity of forming mutual or reciprocal relations. When the experience of giving is also an experience of receiving, the human being can recognize that the other is not enemy or destroyer. That one relation to a (human) other is crucial to the acceptance of all forms of otherness.

Mutuality is not a word which settles the whole matter because this word, too, admits of variety of degree. At one end of the spectrum, a human being can exist as coerced and directed from the outside. At the other end, two people may constantly interact and the action/receptivity of the two is greater than that of each separately considered. My reference in the previous sentence is to two people because this is the most obvious example to point out. When we go above two people the question of mutuality becomes incredibly complex. However, that is just where the search for community carries us. That is, along with the question of degrees of mutuality we must consider the size of actually existing communities.

I have indicated that to be a practical, working demonstration, a community would have to be a quite small number of people. That number would be smaller than was usually assumed before this century. On the other hand, two is usually too small a number to be called a community. The numbers are not arbitrary. A human being exists in the space and time of bodiliness. Given a large number of people it becomes a mathematical impossibility to have a matrix of mutual realtionships. That fact does not exclude the possibility of mutual relationships with any number of individuals at some time. But at any one stage of a person's life there are only so many people to whom one can be intimately related. Even if the number is higher than most of us with our lack of imaginations suppose, the number is still small.

On the other hand, the human race has usually recognized that the bond between only two people is not self-sufficient. The best known form of this relation, of course, has been the marriage of a man and a woman. In times past it was assumed that this relation of two functioned within a social or communal context. There was also the presumption that a love between a man and a woman would result in a third, fourth and fifth. Friendships of all kind were assumed to be part of a set of social relationships. Assumptions about marriage and family are being questioned today and there may be room for change. There may have been a sound instinct at work here which should not lightly be discarded.

Community emerged as a central topic of sociological writing in the late nineteenth century. A contrast was drawn by Ferdinand Toennies between community and society.[4] This opposition between two forms of human grouping is still with us today. Toennies saw community as intimate sharing based on the folkways and mores of primary groups; society, in contrast, was based on impersonal, logical, contractual relationships. As so often happens, attentiveness to the theme of community appeared with the fear of its disappearance. The model for community thinking, the village gathered around its "common," was beginning to be threatened by extinction. Urbanization of the earth, a twentieth century movement, was undercutting the folkways of the village community.

The threat was and is real but the problem could have been dealt with more imaginatively. To have set village against city, smallness against bigness, person against machine, was to misconceive the problem and guarantee defeat. The process of urbanization did become destructive of community but not through the creation of large cities. What developed instead of either villages or cities was endless sprawl of highways, houses and hamburger stands. Large cities that had efficient transportation, low-cost housing and adequate sanitary systems would have been the natural setting for the modern version of community. In a few large and old cities there can be found some experience of community. Unfortunately, most U.S. cities can hardly be called cities since they lack the human dimensions that were the marks of a city: diversity and mixing of people, artistic and cultural activity, participation in political life. More often the city has become a place to drive to and from work while one's life exists in the suburban encirclement. The suburban "town" is no more like the nineteenth century village than the modern urban core is a medieval city.

At least part of the problem is the misunderstanding of size. The human being is indeed incapable of mutual relationships with millions of people. The fact is, however, that it is also impossible to maintain hundreds of such relations. The small village was not the ideal community either, but it did provide a sense of the manageability of life, thus allowing people to work out a few personal relationships. But the small village was also illusory, because life was never as manageable as the village pretended. And to the extent that it did in fact cut out the rest of the world the village smothered what was good within itself. For the individual in the small village, fleeing to the city could be as destructive or worse. Especially in the last quarter-century, the individual making the flight to the city was likely to be met by someone fleeing in the opposite direction.

The desirable thing would be to preserve or recreate the village's intimate grouping in the middle of the great metropolis. We are hindered by the presumed split in the world between urban and rural when they are in fact more on the same side than opposites. We are also hindered by the presumed split between micro and macro settlements while in fact any large human settlement needs a cellular structure and every small group exists in a macro world. The tragedy is that we can end up with neither countryside nor city, neither small nor large human settlements, but with an inhuman mess.

As a comment on size I would like to cite one example of the contemporary search for a community. Kathleen Kinkade's *A Walden Two Experiment* is a candid and detailed account of one attempt.[5] The size of this particular group has varied but they had about forty people when the book was written. Their aim is to reach one thousand people, modeling their organization upon B. F. Skinner's Walden II. The choice to follow Skinner is a peculiar one because, at least in my terminology, Skinner's writing is antithetical to the concept of community. In his extraordinary dismissal of what people have sought for under the banner of freedom and dignity, Skinner would have to include community.[6] There is in Skinner's work no sensitivity to or perhaps no awareness of community as an issue. Everything is in terms of individual and society. Perhaps his elimination of community can be called brutally realistic. Both liberal and conservative politicians have been willing to pit individual against society. Skinner is being consistent with those widely accepted principles, a tactic which makes him a dangerous foe to conservative and liberal alike.

The use of Skinnerian ideas is consistent with a group of forty or one thousand people that wishes to be a self-sufficient alternative to contemporary U.S. society. Although it is possible to call that a community, it is community which is lacking. The resulting arrangement may provide needed space for individuals, it may be a better society than most other things available; but a community it is not. The number forty is an unworkable number to form a group of interaction. When a group has forty or one hundred and forty members there invariably arises the need to impose a system of rules and of instructions by superiors. In Twin Oaks two members spent two days per week preparing the work schedule for everyone. That is a case of bureaucracy having returned minus the efficiency of bureaucracy. An alternative social system is also doubtful if you are spending three hundred dollars a month on cars and some members are working for the minimum wage in a neighboring city.[7]

What I am most concerned with as community is not an alternative social system but an alternative component of the larger society. A community that is a team or group would not solve every problem but it would also not pretend to. Community is not the answer to all political problems but it is one of the prerequisites of coping with those problems.

Thomas Jefferson increasingly realized during his life that the future of the country depended on the small communal unit. In a letter to John Cartwright in 1824 he wrote "As Cato concluded every speech with the words *Carthago delenda est,* so do I every opinion with the injunction 'divide the counties into wards.' " [8] The cell or council is the building block of government by the people, of the people, for the people. Without functioning communities a democracy is actually a dictatorship from the top or a rule of mindlessness from below. Unfortunately, in U.S. history conservative tradition has either defended "states rights" or lavishly praised the family. Meanwhile, the state hardly functions at all and certainly not as a community. The family of this century also does not function as the microcosm of human reality.

A small-size group does not guarantee a community but a large number of people almost certainly precludes it. Robert Townsend, commenting on Ralph Nader's success in working with groups of eight to eleven people, has written: "Nader seems to be the only person in the country who understood what Jesus Christ showed, namely, that when you have twelve you have one too many." [9] I would not wish to set eleven as an absolute upper limit but at that point one is approaching a general limit of workability. In previous writing I have used two criteria for the size of a community: (1) that the absence of one member is *felt* by the others; (2) that one multi-poled conversation is possible. As the cell expands the choice becomes fissure or cancer.

Anyone who has ever been in charge of a meeting knows that with a few dozen or a few hundred people, rules of procedure and chairpersons become necessary. I have no opposition to rules of procedure but the meaning of community is at another level which precedes rules and institutional roles. "No man," wrote Edmund Burke, "was ever attached by a sense of pride, partiality, or real affection to a description of square measurements." [10] Burke believed that we move from the family, to the neighborhood council and then to provincial connections.

In citing the limitations of the contemporary U.S. family I am not belittling its continued importance. Each person exists at all because he or she was loved by a mother or another familial person. When the word community is used, the one experience which the majority of people can refer to is family experience. In that case we know what it is like to put up with someone's faults as well as virtues and the involvement is tested over a long period of life. Getting together and "experiencing community" for a weekend, however intensely, is not equivalent to living next to someone for years, sharing the ups and downs, joys and fears, hopes and risks. Every married person and every parent knows what the issue is even if they have not had much success. Some writing on community and some attempts at founding new communities seem blithely to disregard this experience of the human race.

Although the family is some of the best experience of community we have, the contemporary institution of marriage/family is rather narrow and rigid. Family has to be saved from itself both by widening the concept of family and by providing alternative forms of community experience. In regard to the latter, the word community has to be freed from too narrow a meaning of "living together." In one sense community does mean living together (sharing life) but not necessarily in the common meaning that phrase has, that is, sharing a single household. There are many bases on which a group can be organized; a common household is only one of them. Certainly, as I have indicated, sharing the same house, the same room, the same bed are real tests of our professed care, concern and sympathy for another. But these and other characteristics of human mutuality do not by definition include a common domicile. The strongest personal support for one's life could even come from somebody one seldom sees. I would be skeptical of any experience of community that did not involve some mutual risk. Financial risk is often a very good test of community. However, there are other kinds of risks besides financial ones.

The preceding paragraph refers to tasks or interests around which a group might be organized. A community does not exist for the purpose of accomplishing a task outside itself. My use of the term community makes it a value in itself. Nevertheless, some task or interest is usually the reference point in the gathering together of a group. I would not call a work team or "task force" a community but the members of such a group may indeed experience what community means.

There is a paradox here which is widely sensed but not very well articulated. People who get together for the express purpose of being a community and nothing else usually do not find what they are looking for. In contrast, people who are concentrating on getting an important job done often discover what they were not looking for, namely, a sense of community. The paradox is not so surprising as it might first seem. People who say they are looking for community are often trying to compensate for their aloneness with a few other people who can never supply that compensation. On the other hand, a group of people who are ready to cooperate in getting something worthwhile accomplished are implicitly working on the premise that each microcosm has to move in the direction of the ideal and universal community.

Each of the verbs currently used with reference to community can easily hide this paradox. Does one "discover" community or "build" community? The answer would seem to lie hidden beneath both words. Discover is a word which implies that it is all there already. There might be illusion in simply letting it happen spontaneously. If it does not happen then there follow all kinds of soul search-ing. The positive side of discover is that the word does point to the fact that community as the ideal toward which the race strives is not invented, imposed or constructed. It is what emerges if human beings can meet each other on human terms.

The meeting together as human is not so easy. Humans exist as definite, limited beings in a bodily environment. The ideal does not realize itself without considerable de-sign of conditions. One does not exactly build or make community but one does make the conditions or build the forms. Thus, there is some legitimacy to the word build although it is still not the best word here. One "grows" the forms of community since the conditions are more or-ganic than mechanical. Having a task beyond the group is one way of giving time, water and indirect sunlight to those conditions so that they may grow.

The strength and significance of the small group lies in that organic kneading together of personal life. There is a peculiar kind of strength in resiliency, flexibility and rhythm; a personal group is deceptively powerful. A group of six is not five more than one; it is more like six hun-dred times one. In a group of six there are hundreds of interlocking relations constituting a different kind of reality from the individual. For the individual person the group supplies two urgent needs: (1) The group provides personal intimacy and identity. When things go well the group is the context for keeping a sense of proportion and a sense of humor. When things go badly the group pro-vides assurance to the individual that she or he is not crazy. (2) The group is a social, political and economic lever. Not every group intends to function as a revolu-tionary cell but any group that does exist is in fact some threat to antihuman systems. The power of small, well-coordinated teams is almost unlimited. "Ten men acting together can make a hundred thousand tremble apart" (Mirabeau).

3

Before turning to other aspects of the small group, I wish to introduce here some comments about the "intermediary association." Between the actual community and the desired ideal there stand organizations, institutions and associations. The role is filled by a great variety of economic, political, social, educational and religious institutions. The function of these institutions is to support the existence of communal life and keep it moving toward the greater community. For example, a federal government of the United States is to be Janus-faced: supporting the personal/communal life of the people at the grass roots while at the same time—and for the sake of those very communities—looking to an international or transnational community ideal. The temptation of such an institution is to treat itself as an end in itself. Its pretensions should be modest; for the double meaning of community it is too small for one thing, too large for another. Not to love one's country is a sickness but to think that one's country can do no wrong is a more dangerous sickness. Similarly, a Catholic Christian community of a few friends is nearly a contradiction in terms; the large institution is a necessity. However, to identify the existing Roman Catholic church with the "kingdom of God" would be irreligious.

The intermediary association is not supposed to be anything other than an expeditious means. It cannot supply us with the basic experience of communality nor the ultimate vision of life. Some of the attacks upon or disappointment with such an institution are misplaced frustrations. If we could concentrate on economic institutions serving us economically and political apparatus dealing with political problems, we might get on with things more efficiently and more effectively. Some people expect the worldwide ecclesiastic institution to be immediately and totally personal as if impersonal structures were bad. Churchmen have a funny way of referring to the church as "she," a personalization that covers over a tinge of manipulation. A worldwide institution is not a she but an it. If it would use more efficient and open ways of doing things it might cultivate a life of communities and it could join with others in quest of the universal community.

The joining of the small communities into a pattern of "federation" is the task of intermediary social, political and religious organizations.[11] There are other forms that associations can legitimately have, especially in the business world. But for a religious body the institutional form has to be federation, that is, the vesting of limited power at the center by a circle of small cells. Only by the relation of federation can the small community be saved both from absorption by large institutions and from suffocation through introversion. I will reserve until the last chapter a description of the federation of religious communities.

4

The small group is what provides the practical possibility of demonstrating the fact of mutuality. Even if badly done and riddled with failure, the demonstration is still the key to human life. The existence of mutual relationships of human love is testimony in the flesh that unity and differences are compatible, indeed, that unity of self and unity with the race grow together and they grow with the differ-

ences. The greater the human unity of two, the greater
becomes their distinctiveness of personality. Unity brings
about differentiation.

It is not necessary to have perfectly formed groups of
six, eight or ten people. Most of us belong to various
groups and the groups often overlap. For some people one
group is undoubtedly primary. For other people it may not
be so clear anymore that one group is primary and all the
rest secondary. In any case, many people survive not because of what is supposed to be their primary group but on
the basis of an illogical assemblage of friends, associates
and co-workers.

The small group always has a precariousness of existence. The fact that it ceases to be after a few months or a
few years does not prove it was a failure. I do think that
human relations move in the direction of permanence, but
human relations can take a variety of changing forms. A
community that functions well may so help the growth
of the members that the members move on to new forms.
Nevertheless, I think one must be a little skeptical of the
U.S. glorification of temporary systems.[12] The question of
permanence has to be looked at later. More immediately,
I am interested in the precarious balance which a group
must maintain to exist at all.

In the long run the unity and differences of the human
race are compatible; unity differentiates. In the short run
one must be aware of the tension between the two. Every
group or organization has to face, on the one hand, the
risk of premature unity and, on the other hand, the danger
of intolerable diversity. A prison is a unity that is achieved
without allowing for differences. The unity may be the
only one possible under the conditions but it is premature
with reference to the persons. In contrast, many communes have found that "doing your own thing" allows
for unlimited differences but does not provide the unity

that a group needs in order to exist at all. The problem cannot be solved with a little bit of freedom and a little bit of order or a balance of fifty-fifty. The problem is solved, and then only to a degree, by living with the tension of two values which do ultimately support one another, but which involve continual conflict and striving beyond conflict.

This fact of life suggests that even the best of demonstration communities is not perfect. Each community is contaminated by some of the problems that beset the race and divide people. Every small group that tries its best to demonstrate the unity/diversity of the human race has some deficiency in its composition. It tries to show the richness of human diversity but it exists in its own ghetto. For that reason, it cannot settle down complacently congratulating itself on being a microcosm of human richness.

Each community is afflicted with some of the divisions that wreak oppression and destruction. These main divisions can be described as economic, racial, national, generational and sexual. How these five are themselves interconnected is difficult to say, though a Marxist might see them all stemming from the first and a feminist as originating from the last. Perhaps with the exception of the economic, the problem is not the difference but the segregation and destruction built upon the differences. The cure for the problem is, of course, relations that are mutual and life giving: the interacting of black and white, men and women, old and young, etc. The place where such interacting might have a chance is in small groupings. However, the small group often reenforces those divisions because of its composition. Practically speaking, no small group has within itself the different people who should be carrying on the human dialogue. A quota system to guarantee one black person, one old person, one poor person, etc. would probably only make the situation more artificial. Each group has to face the fact of its own de facto segregation, which is not the same as equating all kinds and all degrees of segregation. Facing the fact of something in one's life is the first step in ameliorating it.

Some brief comment is needed on these interconnected segregations. One can read from easily available statistics the maldistribution of wealth.[13] In the United States one-fourth of the people have no wealth at all; 60 percent of the people own only 7 percent of the wealth. In contrast, 27 percent of the people own 40 percent of the wealth; most of the wealth is owned by 6 percent of the people. The last figure is similar to the situation of the world at large. The United States with about 6 percent of the population, uses up most of the wealth. Economic divisions thus become intertwined with racial and national divisions.

Economic differences are not simply a matter of individuals or groups working harder and having higher salaries. Salary is misleading as a measure; having control of the sources of wealth is the critical issue. And the sources of wealth are possessed by a few people who can so regulate the system that the rich get richer and the poor get poorer generation after generation. Economic reform hardly ever touches the systematic problem and sometimes reform makes it worse. The rich give money to the poor assuring that the poor will stay poor through their dependence upon the rich and as wards of the state. "Extreme inequalities in income such as now exists in the United States mean extreme inequalities in capacity to make personal choices effective, and hence extreme inequalities in individual freedom. Bureaucratic regulatory devices may compensate for loss of income; they cannot compensate for loss of personal choice, freedom, dignity, and self-respect." [14]

Other kinds of segregation and discrimination are just

as obvious though we have a marvelous capacity to not see. If people are put in "reservations" then we are excused from having to be aware of their existence and discovering something about ourselves. Most whites were simply oblivious to the problems of blacks until black people became insistent and refused to be invisible. Today old people and women are striving with limited success to have their problems taken seriously. The two are connected, in that part of the hatred of the old stems from their failure to fit sexual stereotypes.[15] It has taken extraordinary efforts just to make visible the 20 percent of the population over sixty-five years old and the fifty-three percent of the population who are women.

The issue at stake is not which group is to be this year's revolutionary fad. All five of the above segregations are of a piece and they mold into a single question: Is the basic human unit to be an isolated individual pawn in a system controlled by masters, or is the human unit to be groups who share differences and discover a way to live with mutuality, respect and initiative?

The question must be carefully understood lest the attempts at new social relationships perpetuate segregation. An obsession with solving one part of the problem may worsen another part. For example, many communes have failed in large part because they were made up of twenty-year-olds. A world of twenty-year-olds can be a very dull place and an inhuman place. The human race comes in two-year-olds and seventy-year-olds as well as twenty-year-olds. A group that calls itself a community has to have a cross section of age or else it is likely to perpetuate the unjust discriminations it is trying to avoid.[16]

Many communes have also tended to be antifeminist. The rejection of modern technology and the return to the earth may help some men rediscover their hands and muscles. The movement can place the women back in the kitchen, cooking, cleaning and taking care of the children. Not that the men actually intend this result but the men are not so clear as they think they are on identifying what is wrong with society. A movement modeled on the good life of a nostalgic past is almost certain to be anti-feminist.

Sexual segregation is perhaps the deepest problem and it is what community can most directly heal. Sex is trafficked between the powerful and powerless in a way that is even more effective than money for maintaining dependency.[17] Sex has now supposedly been liberated and is used to sell everything from automobiles to happiness. What is supposedly liberation may be only another chapter in the age-old exploitation of self and others. Each individual trying to change things is suspect because he or she is tinged with the problem in ways that are outside consciousness. Each organization that tries to help may make things worse because practically all organizations are themselves products of the repression. The split between men and women is a reflection both of the inadequacy of current institutions and the split in the personality of each woman and man.

For most people, finding a person of the other sex is the way out of sexual alienation. But for some people, and a greater number than has usually been admitted, the route is different. There is homosexuality and heterosexuality and these terms are only generalized descriptions. An individual may have one of a variety of forms of life under either or both of these categories.

Even for those who marry, the step does not necessarily include all the elements of the contemporary institution of marriage/family. In practice, however, the choice to marry usually does bring with it the trappings of the institution. A single pair does not have much choice about what the institution of marriage entails for them. Effective choice usually requires luck, hard work, a little money and unusual psychic strength. Each couple thinks that their marriage will be very special and will follow the lines of their choosing. Most people find out that they are severly limited in their control of the situation.

Community, therefore, is not just an aberration for those who do not have a family. The "ordinary majority" of people are also in need today of a community that would give context and strength to their family life. Wife and husband need space and the context of other people to explore the issues of unity, diversity and mutuality. One man and one woman concentrating only on their relationship are liable to convolute the problem and worsen sexual discrimination. In the past, children were a mixed blessing to the relationship: they could hide the fact that the couple were not growing together and that the woman had no life of her own; they also were a link into a social context for patiently working out personal relationships. The reduction or absence of children gives the couple a greater chance to develop their mutual relationship but it also makes more urgent the need for a communal setting.

5

The struggle to eliminate or reduce destructive segregations goes through several distinct phases. When a framework of systematic oppression is recognized, the first cry is usually for equality. The word equality is a safe one for an oppressed group to use and a word which oppressors can live with. If there is any humanity in the oppressor, as there usually is, he cannot dismiss a plea for equality. If the oppressed are polite in asking and will specify equality in what, the oppressor is willing to start working for equality. The oppressed are also willing to start there and can point out some things clearly (e.g., women earning $3,000 per year less than men for the same job).

Success at this first stage leads to new problems and another stage of activity. Equality for the oppressor meant "giving" equality in some things. Equality for the oppressed is never very clear but it at least implied some change in the exchange of power. Unfortunately, since the oppressed have only the image of oppressor/oppressed to work from, what they may be looking for is a reversal of roles. The oppressor also senses that that lurks behind the continued dissatisfaction of the oppressed group.

As the inevitable dynamism of the situation continues, polite discourse may be replaced by a shouting match with both sides feeling betrayed. The oppressor has done everything he could see to equalize the situation but no one is grateful. The oppressed have some of what they demanded but things seem to be worse. Bad faith may be suspected of those who up to now had been trusted. The pain and misunderstanding at this stage of change may simply have to be lived through. The crucial question in the midst of all this is whether some of the oppressed group discover in experience a new kind of social relationship, one of solidarity.

The solidarity may originate against the oppressor but the ultimate test of its genuineness will be whether it can also save the oppressor. The overall success of a revolution depends upon the emergence of this cell, commune or community which was probably neither prepared for nor expected. At this stage integration and equality are no longer the appropriate statement of aim. Integration remains the long-term goal but the meaning of the word integration has to be taken back for reexamination. Equality with reference to certain economic and legal points remains an indispensable minimum goal. However, equality becomes an insufficient description of the whole of life, now experienced in the newly emergent community.[18]

The movement may seem to regress when the group that had demanded integration takes up what seems to be a voluntary segregation. The group is rediscovering its own roots and its own peculiar strengths. This step is a most important one and a very difficult one. A group may not wish to work from its own strength because that quality is in part caused by the very oppression they are fighting (e.g., the language of black subculture). The challenge is to rediscover within oppression itself a new kind of power that had to be discovered/invented for survival. The movement has reached maturity when the oppressed reverse what the oppressor had called weakness (and the oppressed accepted as weakness) and make it into a new strength.

At this time in history a man cannot give advice to women, nor can a white advise blacks. Nevertheless, the common factor in these movements is that small groups discover the specifically human relationship and through this experience start moving in the direction of a more universal community. Without a sense of what community means the stages of social change can degenerate into a buzzing and sometimes violent confusion. The overthrowing of oppressors guarantees freedom to no one. The growth of communities inside and outside oppressive in stitutions holds hope of progress for everyone.

Like the word community, the movement for change must issue in the universal but be focused on the particular, springing from a perhaps unlikely group. For example, it is occasionally pointed out that men are in need of liberation as much as women. One cannot argue against a women's movement on the ground that men are hurt and controlled by the system. There is nothing surprising

about the oppressor having his problems, too. That fact
is not sufficient reason for saying we need human liberation
rather than women's liberation. Movements for social
change are not abstract ideas; they are actions characterized by the decision to move on the part of one group.
Human liberation is too easy to pay lip service to (though
the animals and the trees might have reservations). A
change in the relation among humans is what is at stake.
The change is in fact coming because some women are
refusing to accept the old way. Men could do something
about it but they are a long way from discovering what a
men's liberation group would mean. At this moment in
history the initiative falls to women's groups that are challenging the basic power structure and discovering another
kind of power.

The preceding comments should help to make intelligible some peculiarities of community. A group which
can legitimately appropriate the term community has to
demonstrate that the ideal universal community can be
realized on the micro scale of the small group. If the
group excludes on segregationist principles a major segment of humanity it lacks an essential human attitude.
It is unwilling to discover its own inner life by encounter-
ing what is different; it is pretending to meet life by
blocking out what it wishes did not exist. Its effort is one
of self-deception which ultimately fails and along the way
it will poison relations within the group.

There is, however, the de facto segregation which affects every group. The test of a community's genuineness
is not whether it has solved the problem but whether it is
working its way toward greater diversity in wholeness. At
one stage progress might be represented by token gestures;
with further progress tokenism may be rejected. At one
stage, as we have seen, the tactic may be to use what had
formerly been unfreely imposed as a freely chosen "seg-

regation." In appearance this may seem to be a less perfect realization of community. There is an obvious danger
to an all-black or all-women group, though the danger is
lessened by the very fact of the obviousness. At the moment
such a monochromatic group may be the next step forward.
There is all the difference in the world between a group of
women choosing to form a separate group and an institution set up with categories to segregate and control
women.

Here as always the language must be carefully watched
lest the oppressor's premises are still accepted in the speech
pattern. In the Roman Catholic church, as pointed out,
religious community means a group of women. Many
people sense that there is something strange about the assumption. In the 1960s a few people in the Roman Catholic church started talking about "mixed community." The
phrase was a euphemism in religious orders for a community of men and women. In addition to the fact that
the people using the term were coming at complicated
sexual problems from a very narrow sexual past, the term
played into the hands of the system they were trying to
challenge. To say "mixed community" when one means
the (normal) community of women and men is to leave
unchallenged or even reenforce the assumption that the
normal community is sexually segregated. If by exception
one wishes to argue for a community made up of one sex,
the argument can be sustained. But the burden of proof
rests there and not on those who think that community,
unless otherwise qualified, means men and women. An all-
woman religious community of the Roman Catholic church
would certainly make sense today but its existence would
presumably be justified by a purpose of liberating women
from repressive ecclesiastical structures.

6

I have now sufficiently established a context for discussing the qualifier introduced in the last paragraph, namely, the adjective religious. When a society is badly divided and individuals are exploited by mechanical systems, religion may exacerbate the problem. But where community arises it is likely to be inspired by a religious tradition or else it takes on religious dimensions just by being a community. The difference here, of course, is between the noun religion and the adjective religious. Religion as something that individuals fit into and something that is constrictive worsens the problems of human life. But religious as a description of a group's activity, its stabilization as a group and its pointing toward some unimaginably great hope can be an invaluable contribution to human life.

In a world of division and segregation religion can simply be another problem added to the five divisions discussed above: economic, national, racial, generational and sexual. Religion can be and often has been another division that adds a terrible weight to an already overburdened world. The problem often is that religion legitimizes the order of things and, no social order yet being a just one, religion ends up on the side of injustice. Those people in charge of religious institutions can misconceive a conservative function as one of protecting the status quo. One of religion's most dangerous functions has been to become part of the national/racial division of the world. Wars become holy wars, one's own position becoming divinized and the enemy turning into evil incarnate.[19] The great war leaders of this century, Walter Lippmann once pointed out, were not atheists so much as competitors with

God for a new religion.[20] Established religions inevitably become interwoven with the state and its policies. Leaders of religion and leaders of state come to have agreements; they understand each other.

The sexual division of the world is also worsened by many forms of religion. This is especially the case when the individual is isolated and made vulnerable to the workings of a large, impersonal system. Primitive religion did not succeed in freeing women but it offered rites and symbols as protection from worse exploitation. The Christian movement professed to "upgrade" the place of women and, through ambivalent symbols like the Virgin Mother, did achieve some results.[21] Lacking, however, both an educational and sexual revolution, the Christian church strengthened some of the divisions that had preexisted it. The peculiarly literate, individualistic and masculinized character of Christianity made its structure nearly intractable to sexual change.

Although religion can have this negative effect, there is another side to the religious life, one that is a protest against the sufferings of this world and a search for something better. If the religious life does not get taken over by the state or an established church but emerges as the power of a community its value is immediately recognizable.[22]

I have described actual community as a small group of people who embody the diversity in unity of the whole human race. I also noted that every community is afflicted by the de facto segregation of the world. The function of the religious element is now evident. A religious community is a group of people who, bound together in part by their religious heritage, refuse in principle to accept the de facto segregation.

In this definition of religious community there is some redundancy in the two words. Every community to the extent that it remains a community will have to protest the destructive divisions of the world and strive to overcome them. This is to say that community and religious community tend to become coextensive, though a group may make more or less explicit their connection to historic religious traditions. I do not think there is anything imperialistic in this ascription of religious; the language reflects practice. Groups develop liturgies and symbolism very quickly and they rediscover elements of modern and ancient religions. If groups reject the adjective religious I see no need to push it on them but the rejection is unnecessary once religious and ecclesiastical are clearly distinguished. As used here the religious meaning of community is a filling out of what is already in the experience of community.

This meaning of religious community could include a great variety of elements from primitive, Oriental and Western religions. I must admit, however, that the concept of community is strongly rooted in Christian, and especially in Jewish, history. The insistence that the locus of the religious is community is an implicit defense of the individual person as conceived through Judaism and Christianity at their best. However, a community context is intended to preserve collective and tribal aspects of many religions and at the same time not exclude mystical, ascetical and aesthetic forms.

While the choice of community may bias the case in the direction of Judaism-Christianity, my description of the religious element is more Eastern than Western in tone. I have intentionally given religious a negative-sounding role. But by placing this negation in relation to the negations (limits) of community the ultimate effect can be positive. This distinguishing of two negatives within the positive might open dialogue between East and West.

Buddhism works from the presumption that this earth is

a place of suffering and what we need is release.[23] Enlightenment as to our true condition frees us from the tyranny of our egos. The effect of this attitude is not, as might be expected in the West, one of despair, apathy and exploitation. At its best, such awareness of suffering leads to compassion and gentleness. If things are terrible the least we can do is show some kindness toward our companions, human and nonhuman. In the historical development of Buddhism this latter element becomes more prominent to the point where it stands in tension with the earlier ascetical/mystical side. In this development the Bodhisattva emerges, the Buddha figure who refuses to leave behind his sisters and brothers. One cannot be saved unless all are saved. Out of the experience of the people there arose this more devotional and communal Buddhism. It complemented the blinding light of a spiritual elite.[24]

The Western church has claimed to go well beyond this merely negative stance but perhaps Christianity still has something to learn here. Aggressive attempts at love can be destructive if one has not first learned to be compassionate and gentle. Since it conceives of an omnipotent God who made everything good, the church has to track down a conspiracy of evil and persuade people to make the world right again. Why does Christianity have to assume that it has a plan to make the world right? Part of the answer lies in the form that the Christian church took. Bureaucratic systems always have plans for running everything perfectly. But that was not the original impetus of the Jewish community, and Christianity has at least had some communities who did not see it that way either.

If Christianity is to rediscover some of its originating power it will have to come from those who make no pretenses about saving the world but who are willing to stand with the hunted. It is not a matter of picking out the most sensational protest of the day or protesting in the

most abrasive way. The protest ought to be neither more
nor less than a protest of a community life which resists
all forms of apathy, destructiveness and meaninglessness.
In the novel *The Plague,* the "unbeliever," Dr. Rieux,
emerges as the religious figure. He sees the world as
filled with people who are tired because they are more
or less sick of the plague. He concludes: "All I maintain is
that on this earth there are pestilences and there are victims, and it is up to us, so far as possible, not to join
forces with the pestilences." [25] For those who think they
can do more than that, the first question is whether they
can do so much.

The danger in the protest of individuals is that with-
drawal from political life may lead to a worse political
system. Such protest can unwittingly increase the physical
suffering or economic exploitation of the world. The danger is acutely real as the dictatorships in many parts of the
world give evidence. However, if the protest and resistance
is communal it has an effect upon political power. It is
indeed only communal life which prevents the absolutization of power. When an individual votes no against the
state he or she is liable to be killed, literally or by a
kind of psychic attrition. When a group refuses in principle to accept de facto divisions, their action is a potent
political force even without their intending it. Every
religious community by the fact of its existence is a threat
to the rulers that be. In looking across history for a counter
force to the mega-machine, Lewis Mumford finds his prime
example in the Jewish community.[26]

Theoretically, it might seem possible to have such a
community without it having any religious character. Part
of the reason why this is not the case is the question of
time, discussed in the previous chapter. It is fairly easy
to get a group together whose purpose is to protest a rise
in the price of gasoline or the lack of a doorman. The

group meets, aims at a specific goal and dissolves after they succeed or fail. In contrast, a group whose *raison d'être* is to demonstrate the nature of human life, to move toward the universal community or to protest against the universal death sentence are faced with a nearly overwhelming problem. They have to be in for a long fight and they need to subsist in the face of imminent chaos. They need that maturity which Emerson described as believing what the years and the centuries say against the hours. No group can do that without tapping into the roots of the race and appropriating some of the rituals and symbols of the race. Those rites and symbols which provide contact with the origins and the destiny of the whole race allow persons to be present to their community.

The words present and community become synonymous. To be present is to be in a community; to be in a community is to be present. Presence is a mode of relationship which a person has to other persons, to oneself and to the world of nonpersons. The greater the communal experience, the greater is the presence. A religious community is a group whose rituals and symbols heighten presence. It is not that religious groups are uninterested in the future but they do not expect to plan it in any systematic way. They are more interested in responding to the possibilities of the present and retaining a sense of continuity over generations.

This contribution may seem like a small one compared to the more dazzling claims of futurologists. However, the maintenance of such a continuity is a crucial one. "If the world is to contain a public space, it cannot be erected for one generation and planned for the living only; it must transcend the life span of mortal men." [27] The science which tried to eliminate religion was severing men and women from their living roots. Far from leaving the church to go back to the world the modern philosopher was unsure that there was a world. The last thing that the Christian church should have been denouncing was "worldlings." Anyone who did reestablish a sense of the world was doing it through a religious community.

A common attempt to establish a new religion today looks for a "vision," but that is not enough. The first need is for communities that are deeply rooted in the earth and deeply caring of their members. From their communal life a vision of greater things can arise. Every other kind of revolution, whether political or religious, is dangerous and will increase the number of victims. The insight is caught by a young woman who in reflecting on her Catholic upbringing rediscovers the value of community that lay beneath much of the silly trappings.

> It still delights and amuses me to hear hairy, wildlooking radicals talking awkwardly about revolution in language I first heard from nuns in school, from priests in church: they speak of faith in the people, of dedication, of discipline, of hope, of the struggle we must make. . . . Now, as we come closer together, as we struggle to learn how to make revolution . . . we are beginning to discover the cost and weight, to plumb levels of desperation we never imagined and to see that coming together is so difficult that we will not do it until we have to. The only way to love your neighbors as yourself is to marry the lot of them: work together, share everything, fight together, build institutions to support yourselves, break down the barriers between you. That is the starting place of a theology, a politics.[28]

7

Community is also a vision, or at least the unrealized ideal is available now only as a vision. The vision is not necessarily of religious origins. Religion is more concerned with the concrete embodiment of the ideal; vision is more the domain of philosophers and seers. Religion exists in the lives of masses of people. Even supposing a religious education for everyone, it is doubtful that the majority of people will become philosophers or seers. Nonetheless, education can provide a sense of direction for individuals and communities.

The social sciences and philosophy have to be part of the education which clarifies the religious possibilities. Without this support of social scientists, philosophers, psychologists, anthropologists, etc., there is a serious danger of religions trying to resubmerge individuality. The tactic is bound to be disastrous whether or not it seems to succeed. The cure for the rampant and destructive individualism of the West is to situate the individual in a communal context. The West was not all wrong in the development of person, the correlate of community. And today the social sciences hold great possibilities for religious understanding by the study of persons in relationship.

Christian writing still refers to the great ideal as the "kingdom of God," a phrase heavily burdened by its particular historical origin. There were writers earlier in this century who referred to the "democracy of God," a phrase that seems to have died shortly after Woodrow Wilson.[29] With all of its troubled history I would prefer a democracy to a kingdom but it is probably not desirable to try to make such a translation of the ancient phrase.

"Kingdom of God" is a metaphor which can be understood and used within its limits. However, I find it hard to imagine anyone being much stirred by visions of a kingdom.

There are other metaphors and more lengthy descriptions found in the utopian writing of all ages. To have a sense of the twentieth century vision of community we would have to take account of utopian socialist writing of the nineteenth century. We would also need the scientific/ mystical writing of Teilhard or Loren Eiseley.[30] The poets, painters, musicians and dramatists also bridge some of the gap between our existing communities and our hopes. Perhaps the closest we come in the twentieth century to prophetic vision is the best of science fiction writing. In this apparently trivial domain there may surface some awe-inspiring vision. Few "serious" works of philosophy, religion or science can compete with Arthur C. Clarke's *Childhood's End* for a vision of community.[31]

If I had to choose a single phrase to characterize the ideal it would be universal sister/brotherhood. Such a community would include humans and nonhumans in a relation which cultivates differences in unity. Sister and brother are not perfect terms but they do have several things going for them: (1) they connote some parity or comparable significance; (2) they signify a familial bond; (3) they can include all humans and nonhumans; (4) the words came as easily to the gentle St. Francis as they do to today's revolutionary groups.

Christianity has always talked about brotherhood and the French revolution made fraternity one of its great ideals. One of the reasons for the failure of Christianity to achieve brotherhood was its neglect of sisterhood. Likewise, fraternity without sorority could never be joined to liberty and equality. The slip of the metaphor was a massive fault not only in Christianity but in most revolutions since then. An ideal of universal sister/brotherhood has never been posited in history. It should therefore not be surprising that we have the kind of religious organizations we do have.

> And perhaps the sexes are more related than we think, and the great renewal of the world will perhaps consist in this, that man and maid, freed from all false feeling and aversion, will seek each other not as opposites but as brother and sister, as neighbors, and will come together as *human beings*.[32]

Chapter Five

Education as Religious

The other base besides community for discussing religion is education. This thesis has three immediate implications: (1) For either understanding or reforming religion it will be more helpful to examine religious education than religion. (2) A religious body is genuine to the extent that it is a religiously educational body. (3) One of the two main criteria for judging a religious organization is its use of the term religious education.

We should probably expect that religious education would be an exciting field today. The intersection of religious and educational concerns should be a place of great interest to every human being. In the Christian churches, however, the term religious education has an extremely narrow meaning, one which invokes memories of boredom and mechanical answers. Most Christian people would know what Leon Bloy meant in referring to "that pretense of religious education which shadowy likenesses of priests, stuffed with formulas, wring like seminary linen over young and uninterested brows." The reason for the meaning of this term has been traced in chapter two as well as the reason that the Christian church has been quite successful up to now in imposing that meaning on the

American language. The purpose of this chapter is to
contribute to a breaking of the church's language barrier.

My procedure will be to contrast two meanings of religious education, one deeply rooted in Christianity and
the other a richer and wider meaning. After commenting
on some of the educational elements in the second definition, I will turn to a general description of what this kind
of religious education means in practice. Obviously, the
entire subject of education is so broad that only a few
comments can be made here; but I do wish to make
several distinctions which are crucial. Before setting out,
I would just note that religion and education are recipro-
cally important to each other.

From the side of education, it should become clear: (1)
that religion is a legitimate topic of discussion within every
educational system; (2) that eventually all education is religious education and that religious is not a component or
qualifier so much as a test of whether it is education at all.
I would not wish to make this latter claim prematurely
lest it sound like Christian imperialism. Only after religious education as a term is cut from its ecclesiastical
moorings can one make the kind of statement that A. N.
Whitehead does in *Aims of Education*: "We can be content with no less than the old summary of educational ideal
which has been current at any time from the dawn of our
civilization. The essence of education is that it be religious." [1]

Whitehead, Dewey and others could hardly be accused
of church proselytization. They had an interest in the
religious meaning of education because they were concerned with the quality and direction of all education.
They recognized the danger in an educational system
which tries to be value free and to exclude all religious
questions. Their fears have not proven groundless, especially in a country and an age in which education is

nearly monopolized in a power system. Not accidentally, a school system which excludes all reference to religion becomes a kind of religion itself.

Ivan Illich's use of the analogy "established church" to describe the U.S. school is apt though not entirely novel.[2] D. W. Brogan in the 1940s had referred to the public school as "America's formally unestablished church."[3] John Dewey had spoken of the school as involved in "an infinitely significant religious work," providing his followers with the basis for making the schools into churches.[4] That development was one which Dewey did not intend but one that flowed from the historical backdrop of the school's work. The public school that was to be religious but could not include religion as a topic of intelligent inquiry within the curriculum had to go the route of becoming a church with its own priesthood, myth and ritual.

If religion cannot fit into the public school of the United States it may be because the schools are not sufficiently public and are avoiding part of their educational task. Religion can undoubtedly be divisive in education as it can be divisive anywhere. But if religion cannot be dealt with in institutions set up for general education, where are we to look for help? The only thing that was clear in the Amish case before the Supreme Court is that some forms of education and some forms of religion are incompatible. It was not evident that the human failure was all on the side of the Amish.[5] Other groups, like the North American Indians, also have trouble with the only educational form available. The problems that cultural minorities have here are symptomatic of the inadequate conception of education that affects everyone.[6]

The double plea for religion in education and an education that is religious is simply that education "not prematurely close its accounts with reality." We are possibly only at the beginning of an educational revolution which will come about partly under the influence of religion. There is only the tip of an iceberg visible now but it suggests the possibilities of combining in education modern scientific theories with primitive, Oriental and Western religions. All kinds of mysterious issues are up for a new examination in the area of the mind's limits and the relation of bodily processes and mental activity. Gerald Jonas's *Visceral Learning* is an attempt to transcend our educational biases by looking to Eastern religion as well as Western science.[7] This kind of book being taken seriously would have been unthinkable not many years ago.

The case for education from the side of religion is more obvious and just as urgent. Without the guidance of education, religious groups are likely to become irrational and dangerous. Education, in whatever form it takes, represents a human examination of life. For anyone who claims to have the final answers to life, education poses a threat. This is a fact which the Christian churches do not acknowledge, namely, that religion and education are in conflict. As I have suggested, it may be only some forms of education and some forms of religion that are incompatible. While this last sentence means that educational forms must be critically examined, it also means that many forms of religion may need dramatic changing. Christianity, with its claim to finality and its propensity for fixed formulas, is among the forms of religion most threatened by open-ended educational change. Before speaking with its customary enthusiasm for a religious education, the Christian church has to ask whether it can bear education at all.

Religious education, therefore, becomes both a litmus test of the church's problems and a part of the problem as well. George Coe wrote a half-century ago that "there is no way to solve the problem of the church school without solving at the same time the problem of the church." [8] Neither Protestant nor Catholic churches have been able to face this challenge. The church school is still caught in an impossible bind: to the extent it succeeds in being a school it is often judged a failure by the church. Much of the church's trouble today is caused by the success of religious education, a thesis which is unstatable in ecclesiastical language.

Religious education is a problem for the church but in a way that the church cannot admit. Some people become educated enough to criticize the church and other people become capable of leaving the church. Many teachers who feel they are doing a good job cannot understand why church officials or parents launch a bitter attack upon them. There is a tremendous confusion of purpose under the ambiguous term religious education. Attempts to improve religious education on the church's terms have unexpectedly led to what I have called the "disappearance phenomenon": sometimes the course disappears, sometimes the teachers disappear, sometimes the school disappears.[9] There is something very peculiar about a field which seems to disappear as it improves.

2

For the purpose of clarifying what has been going on in the Christian church I would like to draw a sharp contrast between two meanings of religious education. The disjunction of meanings is for purpose of discussion; in practice the two have overlapped. The first one is not intended as caricature but as a generally accurate description of church practice. The second one is not speculative nor something advocated for the future. It is a framework that many people have implicitly assumed already but either do not admit to themselves or cannot admit to others.

The two definitions of religious education are: (1) Officials of a church indoctrinate children to obey an official church. (2) The whole religious community educates the whole religious community to make free and intelligent religious decisions vis-à-vis the whole world. A grasp of these two definitions helps one to see that there is confusion in religious education because people are using the same words but in different semantic universes.

The following eight points pertain to the distinction between the two meanings:

1. I use terms in the first definition that are not necessarily negative. Officials, indoctrinate, children, obey can all conceivably have a good meaning. A religious body will probably always have officials or people in offices. Indoctrinate, though having an undeniably negative tone today, could simply mean assimilating doctrines of a religious body. Children are obviously a positive factor for a religious body. Obedience can be defined as a virtue although I think mainly for children.

2. The first definition has an inner consistency to it: the agent, the action, the recipient and the desired result are interlocking elements. Furthermore, the Christian church has in large part survived because the process was effective. It would be risky and would probably be ineffective simply to tamper with the consistency of this process. Some of the church's difficulty today stems from changing one or two of the components while retaining the others intact. Reform has not brought about a glorious new age but rather unrealistic hopes and disappointing results. For example, to put adults into the scheme instead of children will not work.

3. The second definition is preferable today. The second is better because it can subsume whatever is good in the first, while the reverse is not the case: a whole religious community can include officials, educating can conceivably include something that might be called indoctrinating. A whole community includes children; free and intelligent decisions can include obeying. The second definition not only *can* include the best elements of the first but must include them in some way lest the second become vague and amorphous.

4. The danger of the first today is that it is far too narrow a context in which to work. The word indoctrination understandably has a meaning of coercion and violation because doctrines of a religious body cannot be directly "transmitted" from one container to another. The doctrines may be true, good or beautiful but they cannot be "taught" to another person. Teaching, as I shall describe it, cannot have as intention that another person accept preestablished formulas as ultimate truths. Whereas the great concern in the first procedure is "heresy," the question does not directly arise in the second. In the wider meaning of religious education neither heresy nor orthodoxy is the intent of teaching.

5. Attempts to reform religious education without the above distinction are likely to be frustrating for all sides. An earlier progressive move to shift from method to content was briefly impressive but failed to identify the much deeper problem. Then the search for "experience-centered" religious education followed. The demand may be legitimate but the terms of discussion do not guarantee any change in educational premises. And recently the cry of conservatives for "more content" drives the problem back into the most inadequate language. While saying "more content," they are actually asking for no educational content because what they really want is that someone con-

vince their children to accept the same formulas their parents did.

6. Liberal Roman Catholics do not help to clarify things when they accept most of the terms of discussion from official and/or conservative sources. The liberal reformers will insist that they are orthodox, have doctrinal content, follow the magisterium, etc. These phrases either have no educational meaning at all or else have a meaning which is educationally irreformable. The problem has very little to do with who happens to be the bishop. In fact, attacking bishops is an easy way to avoid the task of clearing away the educational rhetoric that the Catholic church accumulated around its episcopal office.

Interestingly enough, Protestant groups that have no bishops are nearly always as narrow-minded and control-minded as the Roman Catholic church. Protestant discussions on this subject take place in a field whose words are intramurally defined. Catholic and Protestant, liberal and conservative, are likely to use the same phrases to describe the goal of their education (true followers of Christ, committed believers, formed in the Spirit, etc.). Liberals and conservatives fight over the best way to accomplish the goal but seldom do they entertain the possibility that the goal is wrong or that the goal is incompatible with education.

7. What is described under the first definition is what is generally called "catechetics" in Catholicism and "Christian education" in Protestantism. I see no way in which either of these terms can be the basis of a reform of religious education. The term "Christian education" arose in Protestantism largely as an escape out of the educational mainstream. Neo-orthodox theology insisted that Christianity is based upon a "revealed word": a pure message which can be distinguished from human experience and religion. The educational application of that theology is "Christian education," whose main task is "proclaiming a

message of salvation." All the educational techniques and educational psychology that are put in the service of that message do not make the undertaking an educational one. A conservative in "Christian education" at least has some consistency between the means and end. A "liberal Christian education" would be almost a contradiction in terms, what J. W. D. Smith has described as "an open-ended approach to a closed system of beliefs and practices."

The catechetical movement in the Catholic church was part of the same movement away from the risks of education. Coming later than the Protestant movement and involving many professional teachers, the catechetical movement almost overstepped itself. For a time in the 1950s and 1960s it appeared to be a force that could change the Roman Catholic church. As with the liturgical movement, the official church solved the problem by embracing the movement and further exaggerating its rhetoric. In 1960 the word catechetical was considered subversive; by 1970 it was an in-house slogan.[10] Also, like the liturgical movement, the catechetical movement was never as radical as it might have seemed. An educational movement in the church cannot be successful unless it does away with the distinction between clerical and lay. A movement that was led by clergymen was, as one might expect, unclear on this point.

8. The second definition has every right to the name religious education. I have elsewhere called the field "ecumenical education" but the term religious education is one worth fighting for. What I wish to describe is education that includes religion as ecumenically understood. The Christian church, if it is to have a positive educational stance, has to participate in the worldwide (ecumenical) religious dialogue. The Christian church tradition has every right to contribute materials to the field of religious education. Christian church members have every right to

be teachers of religion. Even the words Christian education could be a legitimate combination to denote something. What the words cannot do is describe that discipline or framework for education in religious matters.

In sum, the insistence upon the second definition is not
antichurch, but it cannot be done without challenging
certain Christian premises and much Christian language.
The topic at issue here is religious education. "Christian
education" is neither synonymous with nor a part of that
religious education. The term "Christian education"
should not be attacked but simply put aside as inadequate
to deal with what we now face as religious education.
"Christian education" as a term already settles what should
be questionable. If one presumes that the learners are already Christian that is presuming too much; if one assumes that Christian refers to the material of the course,
that is too narrow; if one expects to produce Christian
church members as a result of education that is pretending
too much. In contrast, the term religious education makes
no imperialistic claims. Religious can be understood so
that each learner is religious, the content is a religious
one, and the intended result can be a religiously educated
person.

3

The second definition, a whole religious community educating a whole religious community to make free and
intelligent religious decisions, is the ecumenical religious
education which the remainder of this chapter will expand
upon. The term community has been analyzed elsewhere
but the terms *educate* and *intelligent* require considerable
comment. Both are rich but ambiguous terms that need
development and defense. My use of community refers to

the small demonstration project and to groups of communities or the communally structured religious body.

The first thing to be noted about the place of the word educate in the above definition is that its function is to link whole community and whole community, that is, the agent and the recipient are identical. This point is not an empty platitude. Although at a particular moment the whole community does not function as agent and recipient, the community is still the ultimate locus of both. In providing education, the source of the activity and the judgment of its value reside with the community or body as a whole. A group can exercise its will through jobs, roles or offices but these are only partial expressions of the life of the group.

The only adequate educator is the total life of the body. If there are professional teachers, schools or boards of education, they are simply to be the expression of that life in practice. When the word "community" is used to hide the absence of community life and where schools are imposed upon people from the outside, schools are likely to add to repression. The Schoolboys of Barbiana who composed *Letter to a Teacher* cut straight to the heart of the problem when they wrote: "School is a war against the poor." [11] School, of course, is not intended to be an oppression of the poor but it becomes that if the school is not an expression of a people's life. As pointed out in chapter two, the way that education becomes institutionalized is a key to understanding political and economic life. John Dewey, as a social philosopher, attempted to resituate the question of education in the total context of social life. Ironically, his name became associated much more strongly with classroom changes and "progressive methods."

The situating of educational activity in the whole community allows us to see that there are many more ways that people participate in education than by teaching in school. Each parent, candy store owner and retired policeman can realistically be a contributor to education. A distinction between teaching and education would allow us to see the importance to education of many people who are not teaching but are going about their jobs and their life as best they can. As George Dennison has described it:

> No community need want for wisdom. The greatest of minds are, in effect, its permanent residents. Just as some men are of the bureaucracy, of the state, others are of the community. All philosophers are of the community. All scientists are. All artists are. It does not matter how difficult or elevated their work may be; its action is to create peers. And so the authority that needs to guide the educational function, in being local and close to home, need not forfeit one jot of its resources.[12]

Besides being the agent, the community is also the recipient of education. This principle, too, has important implications both linguistically and institutionally. As some people may more clearly exercise the role of agency in education so some people may need more education or more formally institutionalized ways of receiving education. Nonetheless, education is for every single person throughout the person's whole lifetime. There are some skills which must be learned as a child or it is difficult to the point of impossibility to learn them later. That fact, however, does not imply that education is exclusively or mainly for the children. School may be an institution that belongs mainly to children of a certain age but there could be alternative educational forms for other people.

Part of the confusion here is the use of the word "formal" in reference to education. Formal and informal education is assumed to be a clear distinction usually joined to the assumption that formal education is synonymous with the current institution of school. Actually, the term informal education (and certainly the term "informal school") is misleading. Education necessarily has form just as religion implies organization. There can be good environments or bad environments for learning but when anything identifiable as education occurs the environment is formed in one way rather than another. Form can refer to space set aside, time allotted, materials introduced or procedures followed. All of these in turn relate to someone's intending to direct learning. Thus parents could carry on a highly formal education in the home. Schools can alter the formality in hundreds of ways but it would be difficult to understand someone working in a school who did not intend that schooling take some form.

Although I have distinguished education and learning, the complex meaning of formality brings them back into close relation. The word education does carry more connotation of a social and directive process but the word learning also cannot have a private, undirected meaning. Every bit of learning takes place in the context of the communal and social. No learning is possible without a linguistic, physical and artificial environment to which and in which individuals respond. Education as lifelong learning is a phrase being bandied about but what it demands is realistic formalities for all ages and groups instead of the monolithic "formal education" we now have. By allowing formal education to be equivalent to the current school we channel all the money, energy and people into shoring up the status quo. We should hardly be surprised that the result is a society that oppresses old people and handicapped people and cannot find room for sexual, racial or national differences. In education, "everything for the children" is translatable into "everything to fit the existing molds."

4

These comments on the agent and recipient of education have already provided a start toward defining education. With basic words like education, it is sometimes better to say what the word does not mean. If nothing is excluded from the word there is danger that it has become bloated beyond any functioning meaning. So far I have pointed out that education means growth but also growth of a specific kind. There can be a growth which results from oppressive or premature institutionalization of power by one group against another. Such growth would be mis-educative.

An individual is to participate in the activity of a community as it takes initiative to direct its own life into greater wholeness. Educational growth relates specifically to the relationships that pattern social life. The growth and "wholeness" sought cannot be reduced entirely to a biological metaphor. There is a tension between personal and organismic wholeness. The organism and its relationships need an ecological wholeness. For the human organism, however, the ecological system has to include mechanical and artificial design. An individual can receive education in spite of society or despite what is happening to the surrounding world, but education is an issue of social and ecological improvement as well as individual growth.

Implied in this kind of growth is an interaction of the group with itself and of individuals with each other. By placing the verb educate between the phrases "whole community" and "whole community" I am indicating that mutuality is the hallmark of education. Education and community tend to become the same thing because both of them pertain to the establishing of mutuality among persons. At first sight, however, education does not seem to be that way at all. It would seem that there are teachers and there are learners and that the mode of exchange between them is not one of mutuality. Some extensive comment on the nature of teaching is needed to resolve this serious difficulty.

First, because the community educates the community, the teachers and learner are both agent and recipient. This fact means that each person can play both roles. A teacher in one subject can be a learner in another. At any moment in the educative process the teacher and learner may exchange roles. Or more precisely, there are not teachers but people who sometimes play a teaching role.

Second, the overall intention of the genuine teacher is to achieve mutuality but the teacher recognizes that it cannot function immediately. Teacher and learner do not start from the same position but the teacher hopes that the learner will eventually have the control over life and learning that the teacher has. This is what Dennison meant in the above quotation by saying "its action is to create peers." This is what Paulo Freire means by saying that a teacher cannot work from a "banking model." [13] Banks and their customers never become mutual partners.

Third, the two preceding points ameliorate the problem but do not solve it. Even if the teacher's ultimate aim is the freedom of mutuality and even if the learner turns his or her person over to the teacher, is not the activity of teaching coercive? The best will in the world cannot undo a destructive means. It is no help to blur the language and pretend that teaching does not have any such problem. Teaching and learning are different activities. Teaching does not mean sharing or being present or helping, it means doing something very directive toward another. Those who

are in a teaching profession are often uneasy these days
about this fact but the problem is usually covered with
pieties while teachers continue their work. No number of
comments about teacher will suffice; what is needed is a
careful analysis of the *act* of teaching.

To teach and to educate are not the same thing. The
previous discussion and ordinary usage make this distinction. Education is a whole area in which many people cooperate who are not called teachers. A parent generally
educates not by being a teacher but by being a parent.
Of course, parents can function as teachers but this requires the assumption of a particular stance toward their
children. Intrinsic to the teaching act is a certain kind of
intentionality. A teacher directly intends that someone
else learn and takes steps to effect such an outcome.

We use the word teacher as one of our highest apella-
tions (Socrates and Jesus are called teachers) and also as a
description of a profession never highly regarded in this
country. The common element that joins these two meanings of teacher requires explanation.

Teacher, in the very exalted sense of the word, is almost
synonymous with prophet or artist. "A teacher is a man
who has been awakened from the illusion that there is only
one sane, right and legal way to experience the world and
behave in it. . . . The walls of his capsule have been shat-
tered, and rebuilt so that more world is included in his
consciousness." [14]

Although the teacher shares many qualities with the
artist or prophet, the act of teaching is not identical with
artistic production or prophetic utterance. Teaching involves a set of skills, a sequence of actions and directions
to others. The ones regarded as great teachers of the race
seem to have possessed an instinct to use the right techniques (e.g., telling paradoxical stories) which issued from
their self-possession and insight. This fact is no argument

against training professional teachers in teaching techniques but the techniques can never substitute for self-
awareness and insight. At least some little spark of that
visionary power of great teachers is necessary for all teaching. But the main reason for needing that vision is so
that the teacher will *restrict* what she or he does in teaching. The teaching act is a paradox in which the one who
has broken through limits knows where the limits are and
can therefore work in tension with them. "To teach is
not to tell, is not-to-tell, like Heraclitus the obscure." [15]

Discussions of teaching often revolve around two supposed ends of the spectrum: the imposing of data from
the outside or the eliciting of personal awareness from the
inside. It is presumed that the choice of the teacher is
either to deliver information by reading from notes or
else to let students go wherever they wish in discussion
groups. Even teachers who are more comfortable with the
first usually inject a little of the second these days. Some
teachers get converted from the first to the second and then
refuse to give students any direction. Many teachers hob-
ble along making whatever compromises or adjustments
seem necessary for survival.

These two poles which supposedly comprise the whole
realm of teaching are in fact peripheral to the teaching
act. What are supposedly opposites are front and back
of the same coin. No one should be surprised at the conversion of authoritarian teachers to total nondirectiveness;
the game has not changed at all, only the mode of coercion.
Both the imposition of informational data and the eliciting of personal awareness are based upon the same an-
thropological model which misunderstands the nature of
relation. Information (objective) and awareness (subjective) are both important but they are helpful only within
a relational matrix. In all education, information and
awareness play a part but they are not best conveyed by

teaching. Information is available through machines (including books). Awareness is an element of all personal interaction and especially group experience. Every teacher is involved in both; they are the continuing backdrop of the teacher's work. However, the teaching act is centered on neither pole nor any combination of the two.

5

The act of teaching takes place along a spectrum which runs between: (1) the doing of a skill which requires bodily training; (2) the demonstration of a pattern of language. At first sight these two may seem so different that it would be equivocal to use the same word to cover both. However, there is a discernible line of connection between the toilet training of a child and the philosophical profundities of a professor. The first provides the main model for reflecting upon teaching, but all of teaching cannot be reduced to bodily training. The second is exemplified in what I am trying to do in this book: provide a language that would help us get better control and understanding of our lives.

I am not speculating about what teaching could be but on what good teachers do. A book came out recently with the title *Nobody Can Teach Anyone Anything*.[16] The title may be an attention grabber but it is nonetheless a demonstrably false title. Every person alive has had the experience of learning from a teacher. We recognize the experience without difficulty, but we are often puzzled that one person succeeded in teaching us and another did not.

The place to begin an examination of teaching is the doing of bodily actions. How does one person teach another person to sew, to ride a bicycle, to play the piano, to cook, to make a table? The exact answer varies according to the skill but there are common elements which admit of generalization: (1) The learner requires a minimum degree of coordination. (2) The learner needs a desire to learn, usually indicated by the presentation of his or her body to the teacher. (3) Acquiring a skill usually involves a training or discipline of the body with repetition of action. (4) The teacher has to be thoroughly familiar with how to do the desired thing. (5) The teacher must be able to separate the pattern into learnable segments. (6) At precisely the right moment the teacher must let go.

These elements of teaching bodily skills are present in all teaching because a human learner is always involved with the body. Methods of teaching in previous centuries were often on the right track but were the victims of bad translation. For example, in the teaching of language, repetition is essential but not the repetition of single words or rules of grammar. Repetition is helpful for getting the rhythm, tone and patterning of the language.

I am using the word language in a way that does point toward oral or written expression but which also includes nonverbal bodily expression. Teaching moves along this continuum of verbal and nonverbal. A teacher must know the connection between words and body so that the use of words will resonate in bodily feeling. A teacher has to be in touch with the bodily origins of language and the social controls that are embodied in language. This sensitivity applies both to the most elementary control of language and to the most self-conscious, sophisticated use.

The teaching of reading is the most dramatic example of elementary control. Expensive techniques and endless hours are often ineffective in teaching reading. But a number of outstanding teachers have shown remarkable success in teaching people to read.[17] The common element in their methods has been the careful preparation of an environment in which the teacher gets a feel for the words that carry emotional impact in the personal and social life of the learner. By skillfully touching that point of entry, the teacher initiates an explosion of reading in the learner. The metaphor is not farfetched, as Montessori showed with children and Freire has shown with adults. Freire succeeded in teaching illiterate adults to read in a couple of weeks. He started with the terms that had the most intense political meaning for a group. Once the people sensed that this was the beginning of the path out of servitude, the skill developed rapidly. The background work of the teacher was to be so attuned to the life of a specific group as to know the powerful words; a job, it should be noted, that takes not only insight and technique but dedication and courage.[18]

At the highest levels of education it is still the honing out of an adequate language that is the test of teaching. Great teachers, like philosophers and poets, are impatient with the flabbiness and sloppiness of everyday speech. A great teacher shows how to name what is bothering us, describe what challenges us and state where our actions are taking us. Often, the teacher seems to be inventing a new language but she or he is drawing on the fund of human meaning embedded in ordinary speech. Whether one is a teacher of science, art, literature or philosophy, the task is to demonstrate bodiliness in language.

A teacher who has a sense of the whole pattern can pick out what has to be grasped clearly or learned first in order that the pattern emerge. The teacher's job is not to provide the information so much as to give a way of handling it. Only by this kind of restriction is the problem of coercion avoided in teaching. Telling people what to think does violence to their freedom, but not telling them does not seem to help either. The alternative to both of these is the invitation to hone out a language which in describing our common experience is necessarily dialogical and freeing for both of us. A good teacher does not wish to be agreed with immediately. A pattern of speech can only be accepted after a temporary suspension of judgment. The learner has space to get out of the way, to maneuver and to build alternate models.

What should be candidly admitted is that teaching is very directive and carefully controlled. But the admission of this fact and the restriction upon what the teacher controls puts teaching at the service of freedom. Because freedom is often discussed in an abstract and individualistic way, it is assumed that direction and control are negative and are the opposites of freedom. When one begins with "free" as a quality of personal, social and public life, one does not look for the absence of control and direction to protect a privatized sphere of freedom. Rather, the pertinent questions become: Who does the controlling? How does direction occur? What safeguards are there against manipulation? A teacher can without feeling guilty be very controlling and insistent on opening the doors of speech. Beyond the point where the learner has acquired the skill of his or her own language, the teacher does not enter.[19]

Speech is what prevents us from reaching a richer life; speech is also what sums up the richest life. Education pertains to the whole of life but teaching most appropriately occurs at the point of penetrating inhuman control and at the peak of expressing human freedom. If this distinction between teaching and education were made, it would remove the intolerable burden that has been placed upon schools and teachers in this country. It would also place the work of education out in society where education belongs. Schools would be free to teach elementary skills of reading, writing, mechanical training and artistic exercise of the body. In addition, schools could provide advanced literate skills to that part of the population which

really wishes to have them. The equivalence of education
and school has led to a bloating of the school industry and
not a very good education for anyone.[20]

6

The above comments on teaching and language imply the
other main distinction for my definition: a whole community educates a whole community to make intelligent
decisions. The last phrase is important and needs further
clarification; that is, intelligent decisions are the aim of
education. My claim is that education ought to be concerned with nothing more nor less than intelligence, while
teaching and schools are directed toward a more specific
component of intelligence, namely, reason.

In saying that education is concerned with intelligence
one is liable to be condemned as narrow and heartless. Educational writing is fond of saying that we educate "the
whole man." Much of this writing seems grossly insensitive to the delicacy and complexity of a goal of wholeness. As in theology, the use of the abstract masculine pronoun is symptomatic of blindness to real, complex persons.
There is no such thing as "the whole man" but there are
women and men who are obviously whole already but are
searching for some greater wholeness. The concept of
wholeness in much of educational writing is not likely to
be what would satisfy them.

The widespread assumption in educational writing that
learning can be divided into "cognitive" and "affective"
almost always clouds the issue. The injunction that schools
have been too cognitive and not affective enough is not
only inaccurate but dangerous. That schools should be
concerned about the behavior and the emotional life of

students should be a truism too obvious for saying. That schools and teachers should set about to fix up the emotional life and program the behavior of students does not follow. The small contribution which schools and teachers could make to students' lives would be to supply help that students might use to overcome their schizophrenia. The current attempts to increase the affective will almost certainly exacerbate the split. Schools have never been lacking in the "affective domain," especially in such feelings as boredom, fear and sentimentality. A schoolteacher's job is to remove feeling from exploitative exposure by giving students the tools to integrate feeling into a free and intelligent life.

A standard example of what I am objecting to is a recent book, *Facts and Feelings in the Classroom,* edited by Louis Rubin.[21] The project is doomed with that title. To try to put together fact and feeling is like rebuilding Humpty Dumpty. Unless one begins with comprehensive categories within which relations are distinguishable, it is impossible to have a human unity. Facts plus feelings will always be nothing but facts plus feelings.

This collection does have some excellent articles in which authors struggle to get behind the split, but the editor's comments relentlessly reduce the careful distinctions to standard educational pieties. In one sweeping passage Rubin writes:

> The crux of the problem lies in a sane use of affect, and an intelligent fusion of logic and emotion in the curriculum. It is probable that Scriven, Oliver, Bane, Schwab, and Kohlberg would all agree that both have their place in schooling. The point of significance, therefore, is that of balance and perspective. With respect to the necessary coalescence, my own best hunch is sometimes we choose to act on the basis of our emo-

tions and sometimes on the basis of our reasons. What is critical in this regard is not action per se, but the recognition that the behavior is rationally or emotionally inspired, and the freedom of the choice between the two modes. That is, the individual should be neither blindly emotional nor blindly rational.[22]

It is difficult to see why we need books on education to come up with such platitudes and banalities. Under pretense of making hunches and deductions the writer simply gives us a poor restatement of the problem.

Rubin's answer to educational questions is to add a little more "affect." In a passage where he is advancing this solution, he quotes for support a passage of John Dewey's which concludes: "Experience is primarily an active-passive affair; it is not primarily cognitive." [23] Rubin does not seem to notice that the solution here to the insufficiency of the cognitive is not to add the affective. Dewey's contrast is not between cognitive and affective but cognition and experience. What the cognitive needs is not an addition of something but to be placed in an active-passive context. The affective has the same problem as the cognitive because it is the other half of the split. What is needed is not a disjunction of two realms but a distinction of relational poles.

The start toward a solution is indicated by Dewey's use of the word experience as the matrix of relationships, the "active-passive affair" between persons, within persons and between person and nonpersonal environment. Learning pertains to a meeting and a restructuring of the environment. A skilled teacher can pinpoint the intersections at which a teachable skill can influence the relationships. Precisely because a good teacher is sensitive to human feeling, he or she avoids going directly at feelings. The teacher provides the prepared environment in which the learner decides how much feeling is brought to the surface and what remains background.

The main distinction in this area is one between intelligence and reason.[24] Although the following distinction is not generally insisted upon, I see no other way to go than this: (1) because some distinction is absolutely necessary here; (2) because this distinction has a basis in ordinary and scholarly speech; (3) because there is no consistently used competitor to this distinction.

Intelligence is the capacity of human beings to understand the world, that is, to act in appropriate relation to their total environment. Intellect, as the ancients defined it, is the great and mysterious power to become other without ceasing to be human. As such, intelligence is an "active-passive affair," a going out and coming back, an interplay of both human and nonhuman forces. Reason, in contrast, is an inner component of intelligence; it is the more aggressive aspect of human knowing. Human beings move from premises to conclusion by applying the powerful but limited tool of reason. Within human action one can distinguish a controlling and systematic tendency which is reason.

Human activity, to the extent that it is human, is intelligent and arises from the play of rational and nonrational forces. Since the nonrational has reference to feeling and emotion, intelligent activity is by that fact emotional. A highly intelligent person is a very passionate person. It is not a matter of 50 percent emotion, 50 percent reason. Life is 100 percent emotion but the guide of emotion is reason. It is simply false to say that sometimes we act from reason and sometimes from emotion. One can act emotionally to the near exclusion of reason but that is to act irrationally. And by definition, it is impossible for a human to act without emotion; the question is the integration of feeling in an intelligent life.

What is the justification for this distinction? Intelligence, intellect and intellectual are still the words which can encompass all the data. Reason, rational and reasonable are strong words but not as encompassing. To say that something is unintelligent would always be negative while to speak of something as nonrational can be a positive description. Intellectual or intellectualistic do not get wide usage as terms of opprobrium; in the United States they are largely confined to reactionary groups. In contrast, rationalism and rationalistic are widely recognized as descriptions of a narrow, naive attempt to resolve human problems by conceptual systems. The cure for rationalism is not the addition of feeling (those two can be a dangerous pair) but the situating of reason in the context of intelligence (whose hallmarks are receptivity, self-criticism, humor and peaceful discontent).

Antiintellectualism has been an all too common trait both in the United States and in the Christian churches.[25] Educational and church writing are the last places we need for attacks upon education as too intellectual. Much educational writing recognizes that there is something wrong with our feelings toward life. But schools will worsen the problem by trying to clear away everything but feeling or trying to get a balance of thought and feeling. Every human act is one of thinking/feeling. Thought can be obstructive by misdirecting feeling. The direct way for a teacher to change that is to change speech so that it works more effectively to communicate what we think/feel. The aim of education, in contrast to teaching, is to keep open and growing a wider spectrum of feeling, a greater imagination, a heightened consciousness—in short, an intelligent life.

It is precisely the distinction between reason and intelligence which creates a space for religious education. If education is for intelligence and intelligence is the highest human capacity, what would religious education be directed toward? My answer is twofold: (1) In the long run education and religious education are the same: both are a quest for the full realization of intelligence. (2) In the short term, religious education is the plea for intelligence beyond reason. Anything can be included within religious education that resists the fatigue of reason and its tendency to settle down and declare the system complete. The resistance may be ridiculed by those whose categories are fact and feeling, but there is another whole tradition of the human race that knows there is more. "To see and to have seen that Vision," wrote Plotinus, "is reason no longer. It is more than reason, before reason, and after reason, as is also the vision which is seen." [26]

7

What this principle of religious education means in practice varies according to an individual's stage of growth and the surrounding conditions. But the need to negate imposed limits of life is present for each person at every age. Wherever there is education there can and should be religious education. If education is a pattern of growth that goes from birth to death, then religious education is too.

The "formality" of religious education is what varies throughout life. Formal and informal, I already pointed out, are not especially helpful as usually defined or assumed. The phrase "formal religious education" might be helpful but only if religious education is first reconstructed in meaning. In this regard, I would have to differ with a book which leans heavily on this distinction. The book, *Children, Church and God*, written by Robert O'Neil and Michael Donovan, has been one of the most popular tracts on religious education in the Catholic church.[27] The book begins with the bold assertion: "Formal religious education prior to adolescence implants idolatrous notions of God, gravely damages other basic religious concepts and immunizes the child from genuine religious inquiry at the appropriate age." [28] Their severe indictment may be true of what is taught in Catholic schools and CCD classes but that fact would not mean we should eliminate "formal religious education" for children. I fear that the problem would not be helped by postponing the beginning of "formal religious education" until children can make better theological abstractions.

My concern is that, if religious education is kept in a narrow framework, then doing it better later might not be an improvement at all. Before doing it we must be clear what the *it* of religious education is. Until religious education is redefined so as to eliminate Christian intolerance, I am not interested in improving its practice. Unfortunately, *Children, Church and God* seems unaware of this crucial problem. In a summary of their theological chapter, the authors write: "The solution we present will strengthen the Church in its mission to bring the revelation of Christ to the spiritual wilderness that is the modern world." [29] The unreconstructed missionary mentality is painfully evident in such passages. While Christian writers keep making such imperialistic statements they will never discover a religious education that is all about them in the modern world.

The stages of religious education can be described most briefly as follows: (1) For a child up to the age of reflective self-consciousness education and religious education are identical. (2) For an older child and young adult in our culture there is a concentration upon rational and critical aspects of intelligence. Education and religious education separate; education, though not especially religious at this stage, can be a preparation for the re-emergence of adult religiousness. (3) Adulthood is the synthesizing of previous stages of growth. Religious education now means a critical study of religion but also a quality of all education.

The connecting link in these three stages is human experience. Both education and religion are concerned with making sense out of experience and finding a way to live well. "The great thing in all education," wrote William James, "is to make our nervous system our ally instead of our enemy." [30] That means a continuous process of growth, adaptation and realignment of oneself with the total environment. Religion can easily conflict with education because religion seems to supply ready-made answers prematurely. But education can sometimes do the same thing, that is, education in its modern institutional form can reduce life to the possession of rational answers for an ordinary world. This development is almost inevitable when education is equivalent to school and school is the place for six- to twenty-year-olds.

I have in previous writing used the phrases "adult focus" or "adult directedness" to describe education. That does not mean that adults would go to school all day or that school would be eliminated for children. It simply means that education ought to be thought out from the standpoint of an adult and a growth toward death. Schooling will presumably remain a necessity in a technological world, but school could be a modest part of education, the place for raising some of the right questions and providing some of the instruments to live a better adult life.

Religious education more obviously is something to be conceptualized and practiced from the reference point of adulthood. School has never been a very good place for religious education; the rationality of school dominates its educative function. School could indirectly help religious education by supplying tools of history, science, language, etc., which a religiously educated adult needs today.

There has been considerable talk in the churches during recent years of adult religious education. Church leaders often sound as if they were jumping on the bandwagon of the latest "in" thing. An increase of adult education courses in the country is a fact and perhaps a growing fashion. But if the church really wishes to propagate an adult kind of religious education it has to fly in the face of what dominates U.S. culture. A society that does not know what to do with old people deludes itself when it says it has "experience-centered education." A country that spends a major part of its resources to sell products that are supposed to reverse the aging process is not in love with adulthood.

A religious body cannot reverse these inhuman attitudes but it could stand against them and protest in the name of human experience. The concrete way to do that is by providing continuing education to adults and to old people. The doctrinal elaborations of a religious group like Christianity could begin to make sense to forty-year-olds and more so to seventy-year-olds. The theme of life and death, central to all religions including Christianity, is conveyed only with difficulty to most young people but is of considerable interest to older people.

My only hesitation in talking about religious education for older adults is the danger of the unreconstructed missionary mentality. Without a reconceptualization of religious education the Christian church is liable to set upon nursing homes as the last output for proselytization. After failing with children, adolescents and young adults, churchmen may think they have found their true catechetical mission with defenseless old people. Nonetheless, a genuine concern with the experiences of old people and the

provision of educational resources to them would be one
of the marks of a religious body.

8

There is, as I have indicated, a synthesizing movement
in education and religious education, a movement from
undifferentiated unity, to separation, to differentiated
unity. The third stage looks in many ways like the first.
The movement into adulthood and old age is not a return to childhood but it is a reawakening or recovery of
what seemed to be left behind in childhood. The ground of
an adult religious life is the first few years of life which
set a direction for all life. Therefore, concern for an adult
religious education is itself a concern for small children.
Little people and old people have a natural alliance: they
are both aliens in a world that is centered on rational pro-
ductivity.

A child is centered on her or his own body and all the
marvelous things springing up on all sides. The world of
the child is a great mystery play controlled by unseen
forces. Bodiliness is playful and erotic; in Freud's peculiar
phrase the child's sexuality is "polymorphously perverse."
The child gradually adjusts and comes to terms with a
world of objective standards. What many post-Freudians
object to is the conferral of the term "reality" upon the
external, objective and rational world. The step of competent adjustment to external criteria seems to be a necessity of human survival but it is only one step in the whole
journey.

Religion does not have to be inserted into a child's
life because it is there already, or more precisely, the
child's activity has a religious quality. Upper limits of

meaning have not been set, nonverbal symbols are packed with infinite mystery and the gods of good and evil are alive in ordinary life. A religious body concerned with the religious education of small children means keeping open the possibilities of dreaming, imagining, doing and making. In addition, a religious person has to trust the world and love the body. Whatever does this for a child has the right to the name religious education.

Stories are undoubtedly a part of a child's (religious) education. Christianity, among other religions, has a rich store of great stories in its tradition. If adults could tell those stories to children as stories, the effect could be very good. Unfortunately, church people still hammer away at messages in bible stories. The adults cannot seem to grasp the fact that bible stories are religious because they are stories. In the context of many other stories, Christian and Jewish literature might emerge as highly meaningful in the child's life. Of course, literature cannot bear the entire burden of conveying religiousness. A religious community has to be demonstrating a life that a child can grow into.

I would offer as a criterion of adult social prayer (liturgy) that it should keep a two-year-old interested. In churches across the land every Sunday morning the little children are the religious people who protest against the church's claim to be a religious body. They protest in the only form available to them, which is by refusing to sit quietly in a pew while someone tells them what to think and what to do. (They sometimes interrupt their protest for the kiss of peace.) Some adults protest by letting their minds roam, but the splitting of mind and body is of limited effectiveness and has its own built-in reverberations. Little children have not adapted to that form of protest. What they know is that a demand for a religious body has to be made bodily.

When a child goes to school in our modern world the effect is to undercut childlike faith. No one should be surprised when an adolescent "loses his faith." That is exactly what she or he has been taught in school: to examine critically, to judge on the basis of empirical evidence and to avoid as far as possible taking anything on faith. Religious groups often fear this loss of childhood faith and rush in with props of support. The action is counterproductive to an adult form of religiousness. Only by the child giving up the uncritical acceptance of naive beliefs can a more awakened postcritical religious life develop. Adults do not have to induce "crises of faith" in adolescents. What they could do is supply a human environment within which a young person could complete a circle of breaking down childish myths and rebuilding a critically aware mythical and symbolic life.

Education, even in school, could help this growth by not killing all elements of wonder, awe, fascination and mystery. Schools cannot do much for the arts but at least the school could avoid being aggressively antiaesthetic. We could begin by using as schools buildings that are not replicas of prisons. What have been "extracurriculars" could be given more space, time, money and energy. Religious education in school life concerns the ball field, the bandroom and the dance floor at least as much as classrooms. Churches, to their credit, have often maintained some sense of this truth. Unfortunately, they have usually injected a little indoctrination with the music and ball game just to make sure.

The current interest in "values" belongs in this context.[31] The word value refers to all human activity and to the human judgment that one thing is preferable to another. Religion is related to values but so is everything else. One's values constitute the way one lives.

It is a little strange to talk about a course on values.

One would not normally think of teaching values. Only by contortion and abstraction can value become the direct object of the verb to teach. One can teach valuably or one can teach social science in a way that is attentive to the ever-present human action of evaluating. The attempt to teach values is liable to lead to something of no substance and all technique. To value is a subjective stance which is at issue in every personal meeting and in everything we study.

The preceding words of caution are necessary because many people associated with church education have been rushing in the direction of courses on values. They are surely on the track of something valuable. Unless the issue is carefully considered, however, the rush could be for another panacea which will be quickly played out. The result would be to leave many people more frustrated than ever.

Value is a word that belongs to life and to education. A classroom is not a particularly appropriate place for the word. Only under extraordinary circumstances could values become the subject of a course. I would add that our culture may be that extraordinary circumstance in which the normal human act of valuing has been so covered that it has to be brought thematically to the light. Nevertheless, I would think that courses on human value should move in the direction of their own self-destruction. If educational forms were appropriate and if history, science, art, literature, geography, etc., were intelligently examined, then value and valuing would be coextensive with education.

Since education will always have deficiencies, there will always be need of space, time and resources to do whatever is not being done elsewhere in education. In this particular way courses on value are part of religious education, which always is a protest against the premature closing of the mind. Religious education is compensatory education. A religion course in a school can be justified if it makes up for other courses and challenges the school on its purpose. A church-related school would have a religous function if it were a protest against inadequate education and demonstrated that education is not reducible to the currently accepted version of school.

This apparently negative stance is not a peripheral tactic of religious education but the mainstream. Education itself is positive but the religious question in this context is always: Is that all there is? A great scientist or artist is constantly expanding the boundaries which we have assumed to be fixed. Every association with a great mind leads us to negate the negation (limits) we have set upon knowledge, life and universe. Science fiction literature, computer theory and creative movie making can function at the center of religious education. The critic F. R. Leavis said of D. H. Lawrence: "It is Lawrence's greatness that to appreciate him is to revise one's criteria of intelligence and one's notion of it." [32] The comment is almost a definition of religious education even though writers like Lawrence are often condemned as antireligious.

The case of religious education thus forms a parallel to religious community. Religious education also achieves its positive effect through negation. If there is one thing religious education ought to make clear it is that no finite thing is god. What education might find out about the beautiful and terrifying world which then faces us is not especially for religion to say. But if there be a creative power of the universe, he or she will presumably not be offended by our appreciation of the world.

What typifies the child growing up in our world is the split between subjective and objective. There is probably no way to avoid this separation but its destructive tendency can be ameliorated by the presence of a community. In addition, the synthesis in adulthood can be prepared for by a cultivation of both the subjective and objective poles. The subjective side is the evaluative attitude, the stance which a person takes to life as a whole. The objective side is all of the knowledge which adults need to give them a hold upon the complex world they are part of. That objective world of knowledge includes data of religious traditions and contemporary religious groups. Any educated adult in our world should have some knowledge of this material.

Courses in religion have become fairly common at the university level.[33] Religion courses in elementary and secondary public schools are still a rarity. However, there is a widespread interest and a growing movement to establish such courses.

Religion courses in public education are highly suspect among church conservatives. They declare that nobody becomes a "practicing Christian" by taking a course on religion. They are quite right although it would be more to the point to say that people do not become religious through courses on religion. That is not the fault of courses on religion but simply the built-in limitation of study.

One need not study religion to be religious but to be intelligently religious in twentieth century United States it is likely to be a precondition. Teaching religion is both possible and desirable, in public as well as church environments; teaching a person to be religious is impossible everywhere. One test for the validity of what goes on in church-related schoolrooms is whether the same thing could be done in public school classrooms with full academic legitimacy.

The discussion of this topic is unfortunately burdened with the distinction made by the Supreme Court. It is allowable "to teach about religion" but not to "teach religion" in public schools.[34] One gathers the drift of the issue but the phrase confuses rather than clarifies the issue.

On the one side, it gives over the phrase "teach religion" to traditional forms of proselytizing and indoctrinating. On the other side, it creates a weird fantasy of objectivity by the phrase "teach about religion." All teaching objectifies so that the verb to teach takes a direct object like economics, politics or religion. This objectivity includes elements of comparativeness, procedural neutrality and attention to what is publicly real.[35] But far from excluding a subjective involvement with the material, it also implies a degree of participation in the material at issue.

Religion for better and worse is part of the national life. What ought to be done with it in public education is to teach it, that is, provide a sympathetic and critical understanding of it. Teaching religion would mean using a language that would make some sense out of the phenomena of religion and religious groups. The attempt has its dangers but we are suffering from the realization of the danger of not teaching it and allowing it to float about in mindless phrases. Church groups that can talk only about getting prayer into the public schools merely add to the problem. Public schools have always taught about religion by what they did and did not do; what is needed is to examine the thing directly and with a critical eye. In his opinion in the McCollum case, Justice Jackson said that the school ought to educate the student in the currents of religious thought that move the world. But, he said, "It was too much to expect that mortals would teach . . . with . . . detachment controversial issues which arouse the passions of their contemporaries." The problem of ignorant and passionate fights is only too real, but where is a stand for critical intelligence to be taken, if not in an educational setting? [36]

9

Adult life is the synthesis of childlike attitude and critical activity. Here as elsewhere I am using adult not simply in a chronological sense but as a stage in growth; that is, becoming adult means reaching psychological, social and religious maturity. In the sense that adulthood refuses to reduce the world to objective fact and logical reason, it is "postcritical." The adult is rational but more than rational and ready to reconsider the nonrational. What is not rational could be either infrarational or suprarational. Religious matters are therefore not alien to an adult life.

Considerations of adult religious education are hampered by use of the word faith. As I have explained in chapter three, the word faith, other than as an attitude of openness and trust, is not a helpful category for discussing religion. The inadequacy becomes most obvious when the question of religion is placed into the context of education of adults. Adult education in faith simply does not make sense. Adults are not in search of "a faith" but of "paths of knowledge." A religious body has to provide a religious experience, and a religious education has to provide religious knowledge, that is, a religious way of thinking/feeling/doing. The Christian church has an especially acute problem here because it eliminated the primitive techniques and practices that form the basis of religious education elsewhere. At the center of the church's educational activity has been the preaching of the faith so that, having heard, the people will believe. The procedure is still effective with children but inappropriate for adults.

This fact does not lessen the value of adults studying the past of their own and other religious groups. To find one's own path of knowledge one must acquaint oneself with the paths of others. Unfortunately, the churches lose the possibilities of tremendous things in their past because they always want to "teach the faith." Valuable things in the Christian past concerning contemplation, asceticism, magic, silence, death, mystery are not available to people who cannot take things on faith. Ironically, some of those elements are being discovered in the Eastern traditions by those who want no part of the Catholic Christian past. A person cannot be taught to pray but a person can be taught techniques of the body which help to make prayer possible. A person can also be taught a language to express prayer. Church officials often privately say that adults are not interested in religious education but, more likely, they have never had the chance to try it.

What a religious body needs is some sacraments that actually work, that is, experiences which bodily and socially lift the human beyond itself. Built into the human is the quest for "non-ordinary states of reality." [37] If not served by religious experience the search may take dangerous forms in drug use. Of course, religions have regularly used drugs and intoxicants in their sacramental activity. Christian people are sometimes shocked to recognize this fact about the Eucharist. Wine is a good example of a substance used in religious activity, that is, a material capable of breaking through the walls of rationality, but one kept in a natural context. When the substance is not far removed from its origins in the earth and is ingested within the structure of a community, then the drug experience can be positive in human life.

In this respect, religion holds the key to the incredible drug problem in the United States (starting with alcohol). But the solution is not likely to be seen in a society that preaches against (some kinds of) drugs while making little effort to find out why practically everyone uses drugs. The early church may have rightly worried about excess wine at the liturgies. But the flattening out of Christian sacraments to make them staid and stuffy performances has meant that the drinking and dancing have gone elsewhere. Fortunately, the officials never succeeded in suppressing all the "little sacraments."

Aldous Huxley some years ago wrote a brilliant commentary on his experience with mescaline. He concluded by saying: "Countless persons desire self-transcendence and would be glad to find it in church. But, alas, 'the hungry sheep look up and are not fed.' They take part in rites, they listen to sermons, they repeat prayers; but their thirst remains unassuaged." [38] We cannot slam the current "doors in the wall" but only open other and better doors.

Religious education for adults is reflection in the midst of life and death. Schooling may play a role, especially to make up for some deficiencies in past schools. In addition, high-powered religious inquiry can be handled by many more people than is evident in churches today, but it would have to be a scientific, philosophical and artistic study instead of the stillborn seminary theology people are usually offered. The focus has to be action for a better life and confrontation with death.

As to action, political and pedagogical activity have to be tied together.[39] Those who try to liberate others often unwittingly perpetuate the feeling of helplessness and dependence. Religious education is a protest against settling for any kind of dehumanization, including a dependence on liberators. Any education that deserves the name adult requires the development of democratic power structures.

Religious education, as it comes to maturity in adulthood, is the synthesizing of what is best in education and what is richest in religion. Both of these revolve on the dialectic of life and death. Education which fails to deal with this theme fails rather badly, not only religiously but educationally as well. In the following passage, George Dennison is not speaking about religious education. His words, however, indicate why all education begins and ends in a religious education:

> It is not easy to give oneself wholeheartedly to the flow of life that leaves one, literally, in the dust. If we often scant the differences between the young and ourselves, . . . it is because, at bottom, we are turning away at all times from the fact of death. Yet just this is what modesty toward experience means: a reconciled awareness of death. It is a difficult spiritual task; and it lies right at the heart of the educational function.[40]

Religious education at the least ought not to be hiding the fact of death. Death until recently had not been a very popular topic in education.[41] A sudden popularity of courses on death came as a surprise to many people. One might be a little suspicious of this conversion. A sustained concentration on death itself seems a bit obsessive if not ghoulish. Death, like values, ought to be a natural concern throughout all education and in a variety of courses. Religious education would place death in perspective as the ever-present companion on life's journey. Here as elsewhere the North American natives have attitudes and practices from which the settlers could learn.

The intention of this chapter has been to provide a meaning of religious education to which the Christian church or another religious body can relate. The question to which the Christian church must respond is whether it can make an educational contribution to the religious education which the human race is engaged in. Christian efforts up to now do not bode well, especially in the area specifically defined as religious education. But there has always been more to it even in the church. "The vitality of religion," wrote Whitehead, "is shown by the way in which the religious spirit has survived the ordeal of religious education." [42]

Misguided efforts will continue so long as the Christian church defines religious education as one of its minor functions, something good for the little ones. As with religious community, what is needed is not expansion but reversal. Religious education is larger than the Christian church, a fact not even vaguely suspected in official pronouncements. The Copernican revolution of church and religious education will not come easily but the future of a church rests in defining itself as a religiously educational body.

Chapter Six

The Body

This last chapter returns to the problem posed in the first chapter, namely, the larger patterns of organization and institutionalization that are necessary for a religious body today. In the interim I have tried to describe the twin concerns of education and community that structure the possibility of an adequate answer. All organizations have their troubles today and an antiinstitutional spirit seems to be present everywhere. Just when the need is greatest for national and international bodies that would have authority we seem doomed to live in a parochialism where large institutions are hated, distrusted and fled from.

The nub of the problem is the relation between the emerging individual person and all the other forces of the universe. There is an unresolvable tension inherent to the existence and evolution of the human individual. Other than elimination of the human person, the only course of action is to find a way to make the tension tolerable and, if possible, fruitful. Education and community converge on this relation of individual and organization. Community situates the individual person in a small group and places group in relation to group. Size and difference in a communal context are not destructive. Education makes the relation understandable and provides the individual with the means to change what is changeable and live with what is intractable. To the extent that any organization can be called human, its concern will be to preserve and encourage both education and community.

Religious organizations have all of the problems of any organization today as well as some additional ones. The religious impulse more than any other seems to be antiinstitutional. It is difficult for any group to accept organization but a group organized for religious purposes seems to push the problem beyond tolerable limits. Religious enthusiasts sometimes celebrate this rebellious attitude toward organization generally. What they fail to see is that their attitude helps to create, perpetuate and strengthen the worst kind of organization. An antiinstitutional spirit eventually issues in antihuman activity.

One of the worst slogans coined in recent Christian history has been "institutional church." The implication is that somewhere there is or could be a noninstitutional church. Denunciation of the "institutional church" is another of those devious ploys for not facing up to what the actual, existing institution does. A group that is part of that institution pretends that it is noninstitutional, with the results that the large institution and its subdivisions go from bad to worse. The people who conceive of themselves as the "noninstitutional church" are thereby convinced that they were right in their attacks.

What Roman Catholics usually are attacking as "institutional church" is "official church" or, more precisely, those people who hold offices in the Catholic church. But those people are not deserving of attack, at least not nearly as much as the institutional pattern which produced them. The phrase "institutional church" is a method of combining personal abuse with fuzzy analysis. The institution is indeed in need of criticism, but the institution is the church, not a part of the church. What is wrong with the church is its particular institutional pattern which produces class structure and authoritarian concepts of leadership. An institutional pattern is changed by replacing it with another institutional pattern. Each person in an institution is part of the pattern. Attacking the "institutional church" as if it were outside of oneself is a neat way to avoid any self-criticism. The *existence* of the phrase "institutional church" is a clear test: so long as it continues to exist the Christian church members are either incapable or unwilling to work at changing the Christian church into a genuine religious body.

The phrase "institutional church" is currently more common among Catholics than Protestants. The attitude behind it, however, is deeply rooted in Protestantism. There is a "real church" which is constantly failing but there also is a "really real church" which was instituted by God and bypasses all the merely human problems of organization. The church is constantly urged to be this noninstitutional institution, an advocacy which is not merely confusing but dangerous.

John Taylor writes: "When we speak of the church as an institution among the other institutions we turn it into one of the power structures, one of the principalities and powers, in fact; and it is from these that the gospel would set us free. The church can no more be an organized structure over against other structures than God can be an entity over against other entities." [1] One would think that even on Christian terms this statement would be considered blasphemous for comparing the relation of church and other institutions to God and all other entities. More importantly, everyone outside of the Christian church knows very well that the church *is* a power structure and that blithely to dismiss this fact is an abuse of language and an affirmation of unchecked power.

A group that professes "servanthood" and selflessness is hard to criticize because it is incapable of grasping what is in fact its existence. Any deficiencies are brushed aside as accidents or aberrations. Yes, the church sometimes fails but "good Christians" do not. Liberal Christian theology believes itself liberal because it savagely criticizes the church for failing to live the gospel. What is put forward today as a new definition of church is one of its oldest failures.

> The new definition of the church's place in society requires that it should be present, but not represented. The church which acts through official church representatives is concerned with its identity. It therefore seeks to distinguish itself from the outward world around it by outward signs, but by those very signs it accommodates itself to the world around it. But the church which is present is not interested in its identity. It fits "selflessly" into the world, and by this very solidarity hints that it has a different and a new message to bring. . . . The age of the church with its representative figures and offices is coming to an end at the present day, with the age of figureheads, parades and uniformed chauffeurs.[2]

The slickness in the last sentence does not hide the unintelligible philosophy and devious politics of the passage. For any group to be present is to represent something, preferably out in the open where it should seek accommodation with other positions. Every large group organizes itself with signs, offices and a concern for identity. While one may hope for the end of uniformed chauffeurs, one might also hope for the *beginning* of offices that would be representative.

The Christian church to this day keeps coming up with authoritarian organization, a fact that writers on the church never seem to realize is inherent to their methodology. An authoritarian institution is not a temporary blotch on a pure gospel but a natural consequence. The belief that God deposited revealed truths in the first century and that a twentieth century institution is to be modeled on that premise is an authoritarian mode of procedure. For describing a religious body the place to look is the experience of the human race, particularly the political experience of modern times. The life and opinions of great religious leaders are of considerable help in keeping one's perspective. Jesus of Nazareth and Paul of Tarsus have some valuable comments in the general area. I would think anyone professing to follow their inspiration would be working to break down divinized, hierarchical and authoritarian organization. As for the actual working of a democratically structured religious body, the Christian scriptures do not offer much guidance.

The point at issue here is not the content of the Christian bible nor the exegesis of any of its passages. Rather, the question is the basis for legitimating institutional form. If one's sole criterion is the Christian scripture then the institution that follows would look like the current Christian church with its preachers, messages, promise of salvation and authoritarian organization. Democracy is obviously unthinkable in an organization which claims to be based upon a revealed message (regardless of what the message is). The supposed democratization is the injection of democratic techniques into a rigid caste system. Arguments between Catholics and Protestants are minor skirmishes compared to their basic agreement on how to define the church.[3]

The Christian church should not be judged too harshly for failing to become an educational/communal, that is, democratic, religious body. It does not appear that other religious groups have succeeded either. Religion seems constantly to have been caught in authoritarian forms of existence. This fact was obscured in many primitive lands. The paternalistic authoritarianism of the family coalesced with tribal religious patterns. Democratic form was not missed when the precondition of democratic and socialistic organization did not exist, namely, the abundance of products, technology and emergence of the individual woman and man.

Western invasions may not have helped native populations but the Westerners and their religion were not the start of the problem. For example, Jomo Kenyatta is indulging in a romanticization of the past when he writes: "The Gikuyu system of government prior to the advent of the Europeans was based on true democratic principles." [4] The material in his own book is evidence that the religion and the society were far from democratic. The bias against women is sufficient to obliterate the claim to democracy in this case as also in Judaism, Islam, Hinduism and other religious groups.

The strange failure of the Christian church, however, is that it was prominent in the world in which modern democratic governments came into existence. A case can even be made that the Christian church was an important instrument in the rise of modern democracy. The puzzling thing is the church's failure to recognize one of its offspring. The case is not so strange, however, if one remembers the particular pattern of authority that characterized the church from early in its existence.

Similar to other movements that grew up around an inspired figure, the Christian church developed an official style. The officials possessed the fixed and final answers to all of life's questions. Such possession had to be surrounded with pomp, luxury and power that befit God's spokesmen. The system once created is almost impervious to change because criticism from the outside cannot be heard and criticism from within is judged blasphemous. The existing church can always produce (church) documents to prove that the church should be this way.[5]

2

The word democratic has been used several times already and an explanation of the word is in order. I use democratic as the only alternative to authoritarian and both words to refer to the exercise of power and the establishing of authority in organizations. That is, authoritarian refers to a unilateral exercise of power in which someone has the right to command and other people have the duty to obey. Democratic refers to a mode of interaction in which authority is grounded in exchange of power so that power is not absolutized anywhere.

There are many forms of authoritarianism and democracy. Each form usually has signs that go with one or the other authority basis. However, it could be very misleading to identify democracy with one or another of its characteristics. For example, majority rule is widely assumed to be the hallmark of democracy, but taken in isolation or assumed to be the essence of democracy, majority rule could be dangerous. The twentieth century has fulfilled some of the worst fears of the ancient Greeks regarding the supposed rule of the *demos*. The sophisticated dictator today knows that it is helpful to have all kinds of majority-rule votes.

Democracy in ancient Greece was a suspect word. Nevertheless, democracy took root in the Athenian government, which became an experiment for future ages. Their system was not based on a faith in the "common man"; citizenship was limited to free males over twenty years old. Women, children, slaves and aliens were not citizens.[6]

The government of the United States also did not originate as an act of faith in majorities or on the assumption that "the people" always know what is best. The U.S. system tried to preserve certain aristocratic ideals while building into government an intricate system of checks and balances. The theory was not, as so often phrased in recent years, a "separation of powers," but an interaction of powers, distinct yet always related. The key to this republican form of democratic authority was that a central government originates from the federation of smaller bodies. No power is at the center except what is vested there by the smaller bodies and what is directly under their control.

A major shift away from this form of government occurred a half-century after the founding of the republic. Based in part on the frontier experience, writers in the mid-nineteenth century expressed a democratic faith in the "common man." The development of this ideal was perhaps helpful to the enfranchising of minorities and women. It had the negative effect of eliminating the need for community (except for those who failed to be rugged individualists) and the need for education (except for the ability to read the ballot). The intricate system of interacting powers is unnecessary if one assumes that people already know their true good. No lengthy debates of Congress are necessary; the one thing vital is to elect the leader who will be not a president ("one who sits before the assembly") but an administrator who runs the country's business.

The U.S. system did not keep pace with the expansion of the country and the growth of cities. The idea that the country is now a federation of fifty states is a dangerous fiction. The citizen is no more personally related to the state than to national government, usually less so. Instead of giving local pride and personal control, the state is an empty abstraction or, for many urban dwellers, an enemy. For example, it is difficult to find anyone in New York City who admits that New York State exists. Certainly, they do not admit its existence linguistically. For the inhabitants, there is "the city" (New York) and then there is "upstate" where the mayor goes to plead for money from a foreign government (Albany).

The ills of New York and every other urban center have been recounted *ad nauseam* but there is no inclination to take steps necessary to right the situation, beginning with the admission that state governments are inherently inept and destructive. To be true to its founding ideal the country would have to be reformed into a federation of small communities with an organic pattern of urban and rural life through workable regional planning. Only in this way could transportation, housing, health services, etc., be guided by political control rather than by managers of business corporations.

The case of the U.S. ideal and its basic flaws is instructive for anyone considering a democratic religious body. The overuse, misuse and abuse of the term democracy may cast doubt on its suitability for religion but there is no other word to replace it. There is now a worldwide emergence of the demand for individual freedom. Technology, especially in the form of communication systems, presses the world in this direction. There is no way to turn back from the democratic ideal in the political and religious realms.[7]

The word authoritarian is not entirely negative in meaning. At certain stages of development and under certain restrictions of aim, a unilateral power may be the best one or only one available. In the production of goods, the lack of mutuality may not destroy the person because the worker's person is not at stake. Also, in a family, a child is biologically and psychologically incapable of bearing full mutuality; to demand that is unfair and harmful. However, adults in a political or religious body are almost by definition in search of mutuality. When people are lacking in education or basic goods of life, a democratic body may not yet be possible. But simply to settle into an authoritarian form of living, as if that were eternally decreed, is destructive of people.

Authority refers to the legitimacy of power. In an authoritarian system, the person who is the giver of orders becomes the authority. In democratic systems, authority arises from the exchange between people who designate a way of carrying out their mutual decisions. Authority is an *office* which a person plays for a while. When one attacks authority, one falls into the hands of those propagating authoritarian regimes; that is, an attack upon an authority accepts the equivalence of authority and someone. The way to change authoritarianism is to begin by distinguishing role and person and never referring to anyone as authority. Then criticism can be directed at the conception of authority held in the institution and the specific process which puts people in offices. Attacks upon authority are dangerous because where power and authority fail then violence is bound to arise.[8]

In political and religious bodies today the only place to situate authority is with the whole people. The principle does not solve political and religious problems but is rather the ultimate grounding of discussions and decisions. A religious body may wish to claim that all authority is from God but that statement is from a different semantic universe. When one says that authority in a body resides in the body politic, the contrast is not to God but to any things or castes that would be more restricted than all the people. The possible set of choices, therefore, is things or people, some people or all the people, an imposed system or the creative capacities of the world.

One would expect that those in Jewish and Christian traditions would see the point in situating authority with the people. Instead, churchmen often make confusing statements about what God does as opposed to what the people do. When the pope says, "The Church is hierarchical and an organic unity, it is not democratic in the sense that the community itself enjoys the priority of faith or authority over those whom the Spirit has placed at the head of the Church," one is confronted by two different languages.[9] In saying that authority resides with all of the people in a religious body one is laying the groundwork for speech about God, and not excluding workings of the Spirit. If the people do not have control over their lives, the controller is a set of things or some group of people.

Political and religious power brokers do not assume any power for themselves. They speak of themselves as representatives and servants of the divine will. John K. Galbraith notes the interlocking pattern of politics and religion on this point:

> Perhaps the oldest and certainly the wisest strategy for the exercise of power is to deny that it is possessed. Monarchs, including the most inimical of despots, long pictured themselves as the mere projection of divine will. This the established religion then affirmed. . . . The modern politician perpetuates the same instinct when he explains, however unconvincingly, that he is only the instrument of his constituents, the expression not of his own preferences but of the public good.[10]

Some of the rhetoric is no doubt sincere. Politicians speak of the public good not only because it gets them elected but because they have no better abstraction to point to. The failure resides not just in individual politicians but in the political structure. The individual cannot relate to neighborhood, city and region in ways that are politically effective and thus is thrown into relation with "the good of America" or "our country's honor and greatness."

Ecclesiastical leaders are presumably no worse a lot than most politicians. The particular delusion of ecclesiastical politics is that politics is not admitted to exist. If a local pastor or a pope does not admit that he is a power center in a humanly constructed organization, the chances for a devious use of power rise immeasurably. By refusing to admit that the church has to learn from the best of human and political experience, the result is a conglomeration of primitive, medieval, and renaissance styles of government. A modern national government that has inadequate apparatus is vulnerable to economic interests. Likewise, a church that professes to be a unique invention of God and not in need of modern political apparatus comes to look more and more like a business corporation (minus some of its protections).

Nowadays, not even the church can avoid the clamor for democratic reform. The result is the introduction of democratic elements but not to the outdoing of the authoritarian basis on which the church exists. The Roman Catholic church's authoritarianism is most obvious, but there is protection and hope in the obviousness. De Tocqueville thought, paradoxically enough, that there was more democracy in Catholicism than Protestantism.[11] Where masses of people are brought together within a powerful institution there is a chance of their rediscovering a new source of power away from the throne. Protestant groups that claim to be democratic are often simply lacking in organization or can apparently operate without much hierarchy because the group is small. The merging of Protestant groups is usually sufficient to reveal that Protestantism has not been a democratic religion.

Democracy in the modern world requires the federation of small communities into a carefully constructed institution. Neither Catholic nor Protestant churches are anywhere near that point. As far as organization goes, the joining of Catholic and Protestant would be a case of what Harrington calls the "socialization of poverty"; that is, joining two poor countries does not make one rich country.[12]

It must be candidly admitted that there is a tension between a democratic movement and the preservation of quality in cultural life. De Tocqueville worried that democracy would undercut its own premise, that is, the moral, aesthetic and intellectual props of a predemocratic society.[13] The problem is to create democratic government and democratic organization while resisting the equalizing of all intellectual, moral and aesthetic claims. This twofold task is difficult but not impossible. In fact, it is precisely the role of education to work at this distinction. One could say the aim of education is to discriminate discrimination: to lower discrimination against people while heightening the discriminatory power of people.

We have little choice today except to struggle on both fronts. In the middle of a push for democratic forms we are experiencing a cultural crisis of enormous proportions. It is a time, writes Norman O. Brown, "when civilization has to be renewed by the discovery of new mysteries, by the undemocratic but sovereign power of the imagination, by the undemocratic power which makes poets the unacknowledged legislators of mankind, the power which makes all things new." [14]

The religious organization should presumably feel this tension most acutely. If it does not feel tension, the reason may be because it has collapsed the tension and settled for traditional authoritarianism. Conflict within the church today could be either a death knell or the sign of a healthy

struggle for a better church. Some people are still interested enough to be fighting for some of the values of
Christianity but in an organization more adequate than
the one of the past. Malachi Martin does not paint a
bright future for the Roman Catholic church; he doubts
it will survive the twentieth century.[15] He seems to lay much
of the blame upon those who he claims are afflicted with
the American obsession for democracy. Martin has a valid
point in insisting that religion is not democratic any more
than poetry is. But religious organization can be democratic and, in at least much of the world, has to be.

The Catholic church was quite correct throughout the
centuries in insisting that moral, spiritual and religious
values are not to be reduced to the lowest common de-
nominator. There has to be space provided for individuals
who exhibit special traits of mysticism or holiness. Furthermore, each person needs discipline or asceticism if he or
she is to participate in a religious body. The inadequacy
of the Catholic church was in translating this legitimate
"discrimination" into a two- or three-caste system of organization. If the Christian church had some legitimate
ideal for people, then that should have been worked out
with unlimited variation in the lives of all the members.
Instead, the "evangelical counsels" were given over to
"the religious" while most people in the Catholic church
had their lives defined as second-class citizens. The castes
survived the Protestant reformation and to this day there is
no linguistic indication of change.

3

Before considering how to break through this ancient
caste system, I would like to describe the two ways in which

democratization is usually attempted in organizations to-day. Both of them fail because they overlook the most elementary principle of democratic power, namely, that power is humanized only through the interaction of groups or communities.

The first means of democratic reform is called "de-centralization," a word that was almost unknown a few years ago but is now shouted from every rooftop in the land. My complaint is that decentralization is a dead wrong metaphor and that everything depends upon having the right metaphor. Either through ignorance or devious in-tention, decentralization has been pushed as the great ideal of organizations today just when it is centralization that is most desperately needed.

In the pyramidic structure which typifies nearly every organization today one cannot decentralize because there is no center to start with. There is a top—which is an en-tirely different image. What goes under the name decen-tralization usually only succeeds in making the top more powerful and less responsible. The man (usually) at the top of the pyramid "delegates" power to his friends at the next level who in turn pass some down. At the end, ac-cording to theory, the people at the bottom of the pyramid are supposed to get some trickle and to be properly grate-ful.

After "decentralization" the man on top still has all of the power but he is harder to find behind the red tape, the lieutenants and the committee reports. The people at the bottom still lack any effective control over their lives but are now also deprived of services they might get from a political boss or authoritarian leader. The frustration caused by the unworkability of decentralized government leads to the conclusion that the old way was better. The leaders can then say: We have tried decentralization and discovered that people cannot govern themselves; therefore, we will have to bear the heavy burden of taking care of them.

The ubiquity of the word decentralization in educational, political and religious writing is puzzling. There seems almost no questioning of the desirability of decentralization even though it inevitably turns out to be a charade. Pieties are paid to it as though it were a self-evident and eternal principle whereas the idea was just recently invented.

Richard Nixon, in his admission essay to the New York bar in December, 1963, began: "The principles underlying the government of the United States are decentralization of power, separation of power and maintaining a balance between freedom and order." [16] All three principles might be better stated but the first one is furthest from the mark. The supposition of the essay that the founding fathers were intent on decentralizing power is historical fiction.

In the first place, decentralization makes sense only in an organization that has already been centralized and now needs reform. Founders of organizations do not decentralize. Second, the big concern of the founding fathers was establishing a central government that would be capable of governing the disparate states. The biggest problem was a lack of centralized power. The U.S. founders were wary of the twin failures of impotence and absolutization which could only be avoided by centralizing and controlling power.

Center is a psychological image and an organic symbol.[17] People's lives revolve around centers of interest and stability of concerns. Things fall apart, as Yeats saw, if "the center will not hold." We have copious experience now of what that line means. Nearly every one of Beckett's characters, personifications of the twentieth century, are desperately looking for the center of some circle. At the end,

"The Unnameable" can only say: "I like to think I occupy the centre, but nothing is less certain." [18]

Center is one of the most universal of religious symbols. At the center is peace even though there is chaotic movement elsewhere. Religions have consistently used the symbolism of center for the temple and the city and the place where there is a rope to the heavens. One must get to the "navel" of the earth in order to find the gods.[19] The early Christian church found this symbol of centered power to be fully compatible with its own way. Jesus as the center of power represented the end of pyramids of priests and intercessory mediators. All power in the risen Lord Jesus meant that every man and woman was to share in the power of the first born. The Christian church was to be a totally centralized body.

The Christian church never made it as a centralized body but became instead a mechanical pyramid with an institutional top but no institutional center. The symbolism of the center was not worked out in practical, political terms. Centralized power requires the existence of functioning small groups which can rhythmically control a movement to and from their center. The church, like other organizations lacking the communities to create a center, only too willingly joins in the cry for decentralization. Since Vatican II, power has been delegated downward from pope to bishops and bishops to priests. The theory is that this delegation will eventually increase the power people have over their religious lives.

There is room for skepticism about this theory. I shudder to think of what the pope's decentralization of the curia means. An authoritarian bishop is worse than an authoritarian pope; and an authoritarian local priest is a worse bargain still. Delegating power from on high may indeed destroy the system but it cannot bring about the growth of anything new. The thing to watch for is a redefinition of fundamental categories and here there is little evidence of any change. Decentralization of the church is simply a phrase to cover the fact that there are fathers and children but not educational and religious communities.

The second inadequate means by which to reform organization has recently gone under the cry of "participatory democracy." Here the ideal is logically defensible though the words are seemingly redundant. Democracy is always participatory; but this phrase was invented to indicate that each individual was to be thoroughly and directly involved. As such, the phrase stood for a naive and unworkable theory of what was to be "pure" democracy. This conception is unfortunately an antiinstitutional individualism which is neither possible nor desirable as an answer for today's problems.

Participatory democracy was the counter-culture's alternative to the establishment's reform through decentralization. The two are mirror images, one from the inside which wants "to give power to the people" and one from the outside which wants "to return power to the people." The attempt to clear away the evils of complex political organization always has a strain of totalitarianism. "From the axiom that factions and leaders are evil it is a simple step to the conclusion that they must be suppressed. Whoever announces this conclusion turns out to mean that in order for 'the people' to act through their authentic agents, which are of course his own faction, all other factions and leaders must be suppressed." [20]

Those who will accept only pure democracy condemn the people to impotence. People in a community, that is, the microcosm of humanity, can and should function as "one multi-poled conversation." In large organizations such democracy is not even desirable. One of the values of larger bodies is that they provide specific outlets for special talents. A community-based person does not desire to participate fully in everything the organization does, or, differently stated, the participation is to support other people doing different things for the good of the whole organization. Intelligent participation in political life can consist in not taking a direct role but instead supporting one's representative.

If every citizen in a country or even a city wished to have total political involvement, any system of government would collapse.[21] The fact that there are degrees of involvement is not what is to be condemned but one can criticize the particular ways and degrees that are currently available. It is nonsensical to suggest, as Michael Rossman does, that modern communication media do away with the need for representative democracy.[22] Improved communication will only heighten the problem, not solve it. The capacity for intercommunication among billions raises the need for more complex forms of representation and better political controls.

The movement to de-institutionalize and to let everyone "do his own thing" causes as much frustration as decentralization and usually more chaos. At first "the people" will get along without rules or leaders because they all love one another. But very soon there is found the need for a few working rules to keep the peace or even to survive. There is, however, no agreed upon basis for what kinds of rules are necessary nor how they are to be derived. Meetings get longer and longer; the few rules keep growing. The large group appoints a smaller group but that is still too large to get agreement. Finally, someone takes charge of the situation.

The arrangement which began as a loose association now looks remarkably like a pyramid. The development should not be surprising. The worst effect upon people at the bottom of a pyramid is their individual isolation, which the system has succeeded in convincing them is their great virtue. When such individuals start from scratch to build a new society, they naturally enough build it on the notions of privacy, individualism and distrust of organization which they have assimilated. The result is that they rebuild the only thing they can live in: a bureaucratic pyramid. No group is more vulnerable to this cycle of frustration than church rebels. Leaving the church or a subsystem of the church does not cure the mentality which ecclesiastical systems engender. If one's language does not change, it is doubtful one has "left" at all.

4

The existing Catholic church structure is more than a good example of bureaucracy; the church is almost the prototype of such organization. This form for political/religious life implies a rigid caste system based especially on sexual discrimination. Changes in ecclesiastical structure would be indicative of a change in society's sexual thinking. Sexual and religious questions are still closely interlocked so that one's expansiveness and freedom in sexual roles are reflected in one's religious growth.[23]

On this basis of church as indicator, there has not been much sexual change. The Roman Catholic church is an extraordinary example of sexist organization. If one wishes to belong to the Catholic church there are three ways one can do so, namely, as priest, nun or layman. The categories have remained unchanged for centuries and the language shows no tendency to change. There is traumatic upheaval in the second category, nun, but it remains to be seen what this change portends. The simple elimination of this category would not democratize the Catholic church; a two-caste system would be worse than a three-caste system. A potent third force is always to be desired. Some of the women who have been nuns, together with some women who have not, may hold the balance of change in Roman Catholicism. Different organizations and different platforms of change would have to emerge. Organizations of priests, nuns or laymen, even if necessary on the short term, tend to reinforce the very splits that need eliminating. The crucial indicator is language. Until all three nouns (nun, priest, layman) are eliminated, the church will not be a communal/educational religious body.

In the actual functioning of the institution the priest is the fullness of church. Although writers on ecclesiology insist that the church is the people, common usage is more in touch with the operative meaning of the word church. What the church thinks and does is what the clerical system decides. This fact is not the result of a conspiracy of power. Neither does it mean that current attempts by priests to make lay boards effective are disingenuous. The clergy system is simply the reflection of a religious group which assumes that the truth has been delivered to them in writing. The Christian church early divided into the readers and the nonreaders, a split which the Protestant reformation by no means overcame.

The nun in Roman Catholicism is a paradoxical figure but one that is consistent with the system. The nun is thought to be a quasi-priest who lacks only the masculine qualification. In that sense she is only a step from the pinnacle, but that step is a sexual one and it is the difference between all power and no power. The nun is totally dependent upon father for what the church does.

The nun's role is similar to that assigned to other women except the role lacks the ambiguous power of sexual favors to be bestowed. Many women in these groups are rebelling against this role. To the extent that a new language has not emerged, the rebellion has not yet succeeded. The old system is not as obvious as it was twenty-five years ago but in lieu of any new system the old one continues to function. Many nuns claim that they are the bottom of the pyramid and this experiential claim has a basis. A group that has status, protection and rhetorical acclaim but no power whatsoever is in the most frustrating situation of all, a kind of eternal U.S. vice-president without right of succession.

The nun and priest thus constitute the male and female ideal church. They are the fullness of church and thereby are the administrative managers of its institutions. Nearly all of the official statutes of the institution refer to this group who constitute less than 1 percent of the Roman Catholic population. The priest and the nun are the pyramid's dream come true: full-time workers undistracted by mere human concerns; they can devote their entire lives to the company. The only trouble is that the pyramid is supposed to run up the score but never win because then the game would be over. A pyramid whose dream of total control has come true is very likely a pyramid in the process of self-destruction.

Then there are the laymen, as they are called, although a great majority are women. They are the 99 percent who are the consumers of the church's services. They are expected to contribute to the support of the church and to be obedient to the laws of the church. Because they are not church officials or in a "state of perfection" they are allowed to deal in sex, power and money but under the guidance of the (clerical) church.

One interesting confusion in the meaning of laymen is that lay is sometimes the opposite of clerical and sometimes the opposite of "religious." In practice this is no problem since lay always means non-priest, non-nun. The ambiguity in the term has an important historical origin. There were two different phenomena in the early church which were confusedly related and then practically fused. I refer to the "religious order" and its absorption by the official, clerical church.

Christianity began with the ideal of the brotherhood of man under the fatherhood of God. The phrase reflects a devastating flaw in the ideal. Men were to be kept children and women were not really thought of at all. Without a sexual and an educational revolution, no religious group could begin to speak intelligently about relations between human persons and their relation to the non-human world.

Not surprisingly, Christianity could not live up to its own ideals, a realization which led some people to try to save the ideal among a few. Men went out into the desert to pray or gathered together in monasteries. To the extent that the ideal itself was flawed, these movements exacerbated the failure. A religious organization whose lack was community tried to reform itself by sending hermits into the desert. A religion whose great danger was that it would not fully incorporate sexuality started pushing as its highest ideal the total avoidance of sex. An all-male reform was practically a self-contradiction.

The monastery did represent some progress from solitaries in the desert. The gathering of groups of religiously dedicated men in monasteries unleashed a communal and educational experience. An all-male community is severely limited but any experience of community can be a powerful one. The monasteries became sources of civilizing political and economic power. They also were a source of church reform by shaking up a church which had settled into a sexual and intellectual caste system. The church (officials) could not be secure so long as the religious order had power.

By the middle ages the danger from the orders was effectively squelched by one turn: the church ordained the

men who were in the orders. More exactly, religious orders
became organizations of priests. Henceforth, there were
simply two kinds of priests: the secular clergy and the religious clergy. The ideal of community dropped from sight.
The medieval ideal was reflected in the founding of an
order of preachers, each of whom was to preach. They sang
in choir (the liturgy now reduced to the priest's "office").
Otherwise, the Dominican preacher operated individualis-
tically. The modern development on this theme was the
Society of Jesus, an army of highly trained specialists who
did not even meet in choir. Like the secular clergy they
recited the priest's office in silence. The Jesuit was the
spectacular invention of the modern Catholic church:
bright, aggressive, individualistic defender of the church
of Rome.

A few groups of men resisted the concept of "religious
clergy." Some of the followers of the maverick Francis of
Asissi have had a sense of the question. Small groups of
Trappists today are struggling to return to the kind
of monastic movement that preceded the clericalization of
the monasteries. In general, however, the organizations of
men are sure of one thing: they are priests with a little
extra. Where one should logically expect a demonstration
of a religious community in which the noun priest would
not exist, one finds almost nothing of that sort.

Groups of women arose in large numbers only after the
church was well set in its clerical ways. Thus, the movement of the middle ages was one of daughters and not of
sisters. There was skepticism over the foundation of these
groups but once utter obedience to the church was assured
the church became lavish in its praise of the nun. Tech-
nically, only the older groups are orders of nuns and live in
convents. The later groups who went out to work "in the
world" were congregations of sisters. Common usage places
all of these women in the role of nun, one of the best-

formed institutional stereotypes of the modern world. The
Catholic nun was one of the last remaining ideals of un-
adulterated innocence in the world. Many conservative
Catholics became upset only when they saw nuns change;
so long as the nun was there the pure and ideal church
existed. The conservative was right on one count: You
do not alter the nun; to tamper at all with the role is to
destroy it.

After men who were in religious orders had become
priests and the women became female clergy, there were
some small attempts to reinvent the religious order. One
was the founding in the seventeenth century by a French
priest of a group of laymen who would live in communities and teach in schools. Originally John DeLaSalle's intention was to have a priest in charge of the "brothers."
After what he thought was a sign from heaven (his first
choice suddenly died) he excluded all priests. That move
might have produced a greater revolution than Father
DeLaSalle intended but the time was not ripe. His insti-
tute of brothers, as well as other groups that followed in
the Catholic church were neatly domesticated or easily
ignored.

Religious community in the Catholic church became
identified with the religious order/congregation. But since
the men thought of themselves as priests the effective meaning of religious community became organizations of nuns.
These institutions consisted of women but were directed
by men. Religious community and "the religious life"
now referred to the most conforming subset of church.
The people in such groups are called "the religious," a
flagrant misuse of language. It is almost impossible to find
a book or an essay in the Catholic church which consistently resists this language.

In 1970 I wrote an article protesting the threefold misuse of language (the equivalence of religious community

and religious order, the use of "the religious life," the use of religious as a noun).[24] I noted in the article a fact almost too obvious for saying: that the old-style religious order had suffered a mortal wound in the de-divinization of structure at Vatican II. Now was the time for the Catholic church to redefine religious community and begin making the church an organization of religious communities.

The article was widely and bitterly denounced. Much of the attack assumed that the article, like nearly every article on religious community in the Catholic church, was a man giving advice to women. The most recurring summary of the article's thesis was either that "religious life is dead" or "religious community is dead." The first would be nonsensical since life does not die, organisms die, and by extension, organizations die. It would also be nonsensical to say that "religious community" is dead since such communities are springing up everywhere. In fact, the article maintained that if the church could get out of its linguistic cul-de-sac it would discover all kinds of religious communities inside and outside itself.

My statement that the religious order had ceased by 1965 may be true or false; but the statement itself is a carefully restricted and precisely stated matter of fact. The existence of the religious order is a minor issue compared to the freeing of the language of religious community for Catholic groups. The religious order is significant in a symptomatic way because it felt the immediate brunt of Vatican II's effect. The drift away from parishes and sacraments has been coming more slowly but the movement is the same. What suffered a mortal wound was a form of institutionalizing the church's conception of community.

5

In current attempts to bring about new institutional form there are two reforms dear to the heart of liberal Catholicism: the ordination of women and optional celibacy for the clergy. Other churches and enlightened news media presume that it is ridiculously obvious that both reforms should be made now. Both reforms are tied to the same assumption and at this stage of history both would almost surely solidify the caste system of the status quo.

The ordination of women assumes the existence of a clerical class and its ranking as equivalent to church. Women, having every right to as much status as men, are now to be admitted into the elite. It is assumed that the nun is a tragic figure lacking only the masculine qualification for finally attaining the full status of church.

It could be argued that the ordination of women would be a step in doing away with a clerical class and that one must be content with infiltrating the top to change the bottom.[25] The argument is plausible but far more applicable to a business corporation than a religious body. If there were any sign that a sexual and educational revolution were the backdrop of this question one could be encouraged. Insisting on the ordination of women for status reasons is more of the same old system that needs reform.

The biggest single factor on the religious scene is the women's movement. A church which brought together many women has unintentionally helped to spring this movement. Sisterhood has never been a major factor in the Catholic church any more than in the rest of society. Suddenly sisterhood has come alive—and rather dramatically—in the Catholic church. The ordination of women would almost certainly nip the movement in the bud. If the aim is to de-clericalize the church and end sexist subordination, groups of women can certainly do that better than individual women priests.

Women are certainly entitled to have any jobs that men have. The contribution women can sometimes make is to show that some jobs are unnecessary or undesirable. The pyramid with the priest on top is a male invention which places sex (equated to women) on the bottom. Fighting to get a few women to the top is to ratify the basic pattern and leave sexual attitudes essentially unchanged.

The related reform is usually referred to as "optional celibacy," a peculiar way indeed to talk about sex. The phrase is indicative of the narrow base from which this reform proceeds. Like the ordination of women, the concept of optional celibacy presumes that there is nothing structurally wrong.

Optional celibacy is similar to optional uniforms in an organization. A uniform is by definition what all the people uniformly wear. Organizations with specific purposes have sometimes required uniforms. A liberal reform would allow people to dress any way they wish but a proposal to make uniforms optional is neither candid nor radical. Conservatives rightly resist such moves as either naive or dishonest.

The comparison of uniforms and celibacy is not farfetched; they are related components in a pattern of thinking and institutionalization. In a sense these issues are innocuous and diversionary. Who would care whether priests get married? Probably not many people do, except that apparently minor but symbolic issues are the points of entrance to changing an institution. This fact does not mean I would wish to spend much time discussing celibacy but it does mean that the existence of celibacy is a symptom of where a religious organization is and the magnitude of change needed in it.[26]

Celibacy is a word that is strongly connected to Roman Catholic priesthood. Occasionally the word is used in adjectival form to refer to a style of life but almost never as a seriously meant category to describe one's life. The division of life in many Catholic discussions into marriage and celibacy is inaccurate, to say the least. Most people who are not married think of themselves as single, communal, widowed, divorced, etc., but hardly anyone would ever think of celibacy.

There is one other place besides clerical circles where the word celibacy is used, that is, the religious order. But its usage there is remarkably recent and I suspect is an indication that the religious order does not function anymore. Until about 1965 the word celibacy was not used within the religious order for the purpose of self description. The theory on which the order was built was of a vowed life in community. The articulation of entry into the community was traditionally in three vows or a threefold vow: poverty, chastity, obedience. The middle word was interpreted to exclude marriage but all three vows were aspects of committing oneself to the communal life. When the institution began to crumble, poverty and obedience went through convoluted and unsuccessful redefinition. But chastity was clear, or, rather, chastity now translated into celibacy. Everything was reduced to the one thing that would clearly distinguish the group and if that could be justified everything would be all right. But clarity and persuasiveness did not go together. The choice of the religious order to stake its life on that word was a disaster or perhaps its choice to switch to that language indicated that *it* (the religious order) had already ceased to exist when its people first started to talk about celibacy.

There was a consistency in requiring celibacy of the Catholic priesthood. The abstention from family life was one part of the role of pastor *to* a community. If priests were to marry today that might be one step in a systematic change. The far more likely thing is that this change would obscure the problem and patch up a structure which needs more change than letting a few men marry. In fact, if Roman conservatives wish to prevent structural change they might do well "to give permission" to marry. In this way priesthood, clerical class and unilateral power would remain intact. We would simply need a new category which would fit easily into the existing church, namely, priest's wife. Protestantism has done all the groundwork for that category.

So long as the word priest is a noun, the marriage of priests will solidify the existence of the caste system. Although celibacy is a chief symptom of what ails the Catholic church, one does not cure a disease by attacking the symptoms (or making them optional). The need is to change the noun to an adjective and locate the word priestly within a religious community. Protestant churches have already done much of what the liberal Catholic church is proposing but larger or different steps are needed. At this moment in history it would seem useless for the Catholic church to follow a path that has been of limited success in Protestantism. A church that was an organism of small communities would need neither married clergy nor unmarried clergy.

Attacking the clergy would be unfair and unfruitful. There are some extraordinarily fine men who are Catholic priests and Protestant ministers. Some of them are doing heroically great work. I am not advocating that they quit but I am urging that they begin to change some of the trappings, especially language. It is most unlikely and probably undesirable that they all drop from the ranks of clergy. The most creative and imaginative priests already have a sense that priest should become adjectival and that it should be a role within a community. But so long as young men are "elevated" for life to this role it is practically inevitable that most of them will become the role. Despite the decline of seminary enrollments there will probably continue to be young men who want the status. For the transition into a new church I look more to older priests than young ones. There are older men who have continued to learn and whose experience of life has been chastened in hospitals, prisons and ghettos. Anything which provides such men with new communal experience and better professional skills is a step forward for the whole church. The elimination of a clerical class does not mean pushing anyone over a cliff.

It should be noted here that the problems of Catholic bishops are merely the problems of priest writ large. When priests draw a line of hierarchy it is usually a line between priest and bishop. The severest criticism of bishops is by priests and the criticism is sometimes personal and abusive. That mode of attack allows the priest to avoid the problem which is closer to home. A hierarchical church is one which has a clergy and laity; the basic split is between priest and people. It is this division that is at the root of nonaccountability, identification of person with role and a religious form that is verbose, legalistic and authoritarian. Lay people hardly ever criticize the bishop; he is a shadowy figure hardly present to the consciousness at all. A suggestion sometimes offered by priests is that priests should elect the bishop. The proposal cannot be taken very seriously unless it includes the election of priests. More precisely, communities could appoint people to the priestly role who might in turn elect a woman or man to play the episcopal role for a time.

The word around which many Catholic efforts have recently crystallized is "ministry." The word may do it although it starts with a handicap. If the Catholic church is really ready to discuss priestly and other roles in the constituting of a church, that would indeed be a revolution. My first problem is that the word ministry has almost no currency in the American English language outside of church circles. The case is different in the British language in which ministry has political and educational significance. It seems that the U.S. Catholic church imported the word from Protestant churches, a tactic which is not bad but is by no means sufficient. The word ministry is hampered in Protestant circles by its narrow base, which has never been sufficient to overcome the split of clergy and lay.

Catholic officials are also doing something peculiar with the word ministry. In particular the use of the phrase "ministerial priesthood" is a dangerous abuse of language.[27] Is there really supposed to be a nonministerial priesthood to contrast to that phrase? The way institutions totally co-opt language is to take the two appropriate words, change the noun into an adjective and the adjective into a noun. With the two right words one is supposedly addressing the real issue, except that the words have been made into a new abstraction which only the institution can define. If the officials spoke of priestly ministry, people might begin to notice that since priestly is an adjective there is no need for priests. Thus, church officials talk of ministerial priesthood which under the semblance of opening the church obliterates the chance that language will help us.[28]

I am therefore skeptical of the use of the word ministry unless it has a solid meaning clearly different from what priests and (ordained) ministers currently do. I fail to see that happening. The attempt to subsume education under ministry is a particular danger so long as the word ministry has the churchy meaning it has had. For reasons set out in this book the Christian church is in no position to make claims about going beyond "mere education" to ministry.[29]

The ecclesiastical translation of that claim would be devastating to the educational movement in the Catholic church. For all of its troubles, the word education has immeasurably more strength than the word ministry in the defining of a religious body.

6

The religious body might best be described as an organism of cells. The deficiency in that image is the fact that in this case the cells are personal and have a different kind of autonomy than cells in a physical organism. The existence of the cell is a necessary but not sufficient condition of the existence of the body. The many cells need organizing or design. The internal design of the cell cannot simply be projected to the body as a whole. In a small group there is almost no need for rules, constitutions, elections, contracts, etc. In a large organization objective instruments of operation are highly desirable and sometimes urgently necessary. It would be unwise, even if it were possible, to describe the objective instruments of the religious body because the functioning cells have to discover what is the best way for them. At most, some positive principles can be described and some negative practices can be exposed.

The relation of persons within the religious community might best be described as sister and brother. For reasons given in chapter four these terms capture something of the relation. But the use of these terms as titles of address precede a personal age and this kind of substitution is no longer acceptable. One way to describe what has been happening in the Catholic church is to say that nuns are becoming sisters. Many of them are shocked to find out what others could have told them beforehand, namely, that there is no place to be a sister in the Catholic church, any more than a brother. If there is to be a church of sisters and brothers it would have to be created.

Women are faced with the larger burden in this struggle both because of their subordinate role in the past and the rising strength of a women's movement today. The critical balance for the future of the Catholic church probably rests on the emergence of a religious sisterhood. There are women who have been nuns and are a strength beyond their numbers, but they are only one component of sisterhood. If the sisters who have been nuns join the sisters who have not been nuns, the Catholic church would have its hands full.

There is a group of women in (or associated with) the Catholic church who have not been given much attention in the news media but they could be an extraordinary force if organized. They are women of about thirty-five to fifty years old who usually have two to twelve children and have miraculously survived. They are now in the process of trying to refocus all that energy which they have needed to survive. They may be a small minority but they are tough-minded realists, eager for action, and the most intellectually alive people in the Catholic church. Unfortunately, many Catholic women are estranged, on the one hand, from sisters in a convent whose lives exclude marriage and motherhood and, on the other hand, from feminist sisters whose ideology seems to belittle marriage and motherhood. The church's language has exacerbated society's split between sisterhood and marriage. What needs saying with the demonstration of fact is not only that sisters can be married but that sisterhood is one of the conditions for humanizing marriage.

Sisterhood cannot swing the whole change. Women need help from men who have developed a sense of brotherhood. Here the use of the word so far outstrips the reality that the problem is different from and worse than sisterhood. Brotherhoods in society are either a superficial back-slapping kind of organization or a misnamed bureaucratic pyramid which an all-male society inevitably builds.

In the church there seem to be very few men capable of or willing to move in the direction of brotherhood. Men tied in to the official church seem to have no maneuverability at all. Laymen who get interested in church matters often want to play priest. There are groups of religious brothers who might be able to spearhead a movement if their small size and past history did not hinder them. The Catholic church mainly locates the word brother with the nonordained members of clerical religious orders. The sad fact is that in the Catholic church brotherhood is considered a step down for nearly everyone.

The situation is not hopeless, however. Few people would have prophesied the rise of sisterhood a few decades ago. There are undoubtedly some men throughout society who are looking for something other than hierarchy in their jobs, religion and lovemaking. The bureaucratic system can only disparage them for being worse than women. They do have a long way to go but there may yet arise a group of men who by experiencing brotherhood in a deeply religious sense will join women in the constituting of a religious body. When brother in church refers to the standard relation of men toward each other, toward women and toward the earth, the Christian church will have come of age.

Some of the church cells might be all men, some might be all women; some would be cells of men and women. Some cells might live in the same house, some might meet for social, political or leisure purposes; once the language is freed from its captivity by parish/order, there are unlimited forms that religious community can take. While a religious community would presumably engage in prayer, education and social action, each individual may not be equally involved in everything.

It must be admitted that any communal arrangement poses some threat to the contemporary form of marriage. Just as the drug problem could best be dealt with in the context of a religious community, so also sex would have its healthiest context in a religious community.[30] Society badly needs some help with sex, and, of course, the exclusion of sex from the concept of religious community is now absurd. The past record on the question is not very encouraging but we have no choice except to work at relating the individual sexual person to communal religious settings. To work through sexual and marital problems, people need the support and stability of their sisters and brothers.

The activity of the religious community could be divided into the priestly and the prophetic. Both of these words have their limitations, but they have currency well beyond churchy circles and can be salvaged to describe the positive aspects of community life. Hegelian philosophy was basically correct in seeing an opposition between priests and prophets; the two concepts are exclusive of one another. The class of priests preserves the past, concentrates on ritual and has a feel for continuity with the earth. The counter-class of prophets has visions of a future world, is impatient with ritual and pushes for a break with the past and nature. When the priests and the prophets confront one another, everyone else is liable to suffer. The words priestly and prophetic are capable of describing something positive but the functions are too important to be given over to a class of rulers and a clique of rebels.

Priestly and prophetic can go together if they describe the quality of a community's life. The community by existing is the unity of past/future. Presence in community is what allows a criticism of the past with "intellectual piety" and a hope for the future without anxiety and ideology. A community preserves ritual not by locking the books in the attic but by living it daily. The ritual framework prepares for and follows upon moments of visionary breakdown and breakthrough. Finally, the community experience demonstrates that freedom from the bonds of nonhuman nature is only achieved in a tender, loving relationship to the earth.[31]

If the community were priestly/prophetic an individual could step in and out of both roles. One might feel more prophetic on Monday, Wednesday and Friday, and more priestly the other days. One might be prophetic in one part of life and priestly in another part. The young person could have visions while the old person had dreams but each would share with the other; and occasionally they might switch their roles. No one would become the role because each man and woman would play both roles. One of the directions in the life of Jesus was the elimination of classes of priests and prophets. The early church understood that each of the church members was to share directly in the priestly/prophetic power manifest in the Lord Jesus. But in the absence of anything that could realistically be called religious communities, the priests and prophets came back.

The organization of the whole religious body would need more formality than the small community. The large body would use the best techniques available from anywhere to protect individuals, encourage community growth and efficiently accomplish the tasks it wants done. If the communities function—that is, the group members interact with each other and the entire group with other groups—certain individuals would become visible: those with special intelligence, talents, training, courage or holiness, etc. People could then be elected or appointed to positions of "office." The organization of communities could act through its representatives. However, all power for the group would be vested at the center of the group in a forum for debate and decision making. Each person could temporarily exercise an office of authority. There would be guarantees of accountability to the people and a clear, contractual safeguard for the individual.[32]

I am wary of the word leader. I suspect that the word may be inseparable from both a spatial image and an individualistic role. The word leader probably clouds the several different kinds of action which are needed in small religious communities and large religious bodies. In the small group each person's talent can be brought out. Some groups of people are led by leaders but that is the kind of grouping to which the word community does not properly apply. Community denotes mutuality, which is by no means easy to reach. But what it implies is that a community is leaderless because each person is a "leader," or better stated, the competence and greatness of each person contributes to the group.[33]

In the large body there are people who could be called leaders but it is not as if there were some definable trait called leadership. The body does need courage, intelligence, articulateness, decisiveness, peacefulness, passion and many other qualities. There should be forums in which these best of human qualities can surface. We would do far better studying how an organization generates its officials rather than spending our time trying to describe the ideal leader. When leader is spoken of as a single concept the model of it will almost certainly come from the business world. There will continue to be administrative tasks within the political and religious domains but they should be under the direction of political and religious offices.

One governmental arm that a religous body could cultivate is a council of wise old men and women. The assumption in Western society that leadership is a matter of bureaucratic administration either leaves out old people or leaves them in jobs they are no longer capable of doing. An organization does not escape gerontocracy by going on a youth kick, especially when the jobs are not temporary. The real step forward would be to distinguish kinds of jobs so that the old people could contribute in their own way. The U.S. supreme court is an imperfect example of what political and religious bodies need, that is, a group of trusted and experienced people who are not worried about reelection to anything and can be the wisdom, arbiter and conscience for the body. If the church continues "ordination," perhaps one of the qualifications should be that the man or woman be over seventy years old.

Religious bodies should have their administrative tasks handled by an energetic team of men and women. Youth and health are generally a help in taking care of the complex, managerial problems in a mobile society. The administrative team would have balance from the council of older officials to supply the longer perspective. Both the young and the old can be dangerous but only when there is no interaction between them. Religious bodies that claim to accept all of experience are tested in that claim by how they treat old people. Religious bodies have a special responsibility to honor their old people, providing significant and easy ways for the old to participate in the body. Confucius said: It is my ambition to comfort the old, to be faithful to friends and to cherish the young.[34] Only with the means for mutual promises and common decisions can we accomplish that threefold aim.

7

In this book I have tried to avoid speculation and prediction. I have not tried to lay out a theory for implementation. Rather, I have tried to describe what already exists in some fashion though our words are inadequate to our experience. Nearly every element of a religious body can be found in a contemporary or past religious organization. One cannot create a perfect religious body by abstracting elements from diverse religious organizations. In fact, one cannot create any kind of religious body that way. Bodies gestate, are born, mature and join the earth to be reborn in new form. In all likelihood, there never will be one perfect religious body. There will continue to be many religious organizations that approximate a genuine religious body, that is, an organization sustaining bodiliness and formed in the model of an educating/communal organism.

Many people know quite well what they want religiously and what they want is essentially very simple. But getting to something simple is not always a simple matter. The change of institution requires a precise statement of conditions and long, patient work to achieve the desired result. The two criteria described in this book are education and community. Where these two coincide there will emerge the religious education and religious community that are the conditions of a religious body.

The body's community life means an environment of private and public prayer, private integrity and public action, solitude and intimacy, contemplative silence and sensual celebration. The body would be a community of communities that stands its ground in the face of coercion, violence, despair and death. The body would demonstrate

by a life of mutuality that life is stronger than death and
that the unity of all things does not eliminate the richness
of personal uniqueness. For those outside of its boundaries, the religious body could provide communities of
care and healing. Many psychologists say that our society
needs "checkout places" where one can "enter and find
confirmation for *any* way one has chosen to be, or any
that circumstances have brought one to." [35]

The body's religious education means an environment
for lifelong growth in learning. Those who never stop
learning discover that education has a religious meaning.
For those who desire it, a religious body ought to assemble
a systematic religious knowledge to be continually tested
in experience. Toward those who are outside of its boundaries, the religious body would be an educational force
in a nonimperious way. This contribution could take the
form of sponsoring some schools for those who most need
them or running some schools that take the risk of genuine educational experiments. The overall intent of the
body would simply be to keep open and growing the educational possibilities of the race.

The world still waits not for a messiah but for those
men and women who learn to live and to die in order that
the world may be reborn.

Notes

CHAPTER ONE

(1) See Mary Douglas, *Natural Symbols* (New York: Vintage, 1970), pp. 16–17.

(2) Norman O. Brown, *Love's Body* (New York: Vintage, 1966).

(3) Books on church reform today will often incorporate the language and apparatus of political democracy without challenging the basic methodological assumption of the ultimate criterion for reform. See Richard McBrien, *The Remaking of the Church* (New York: Harper and Row, 1973); James Anderson, *To Come Alive* (New York: Harper and Row, 1973); Patrick Granfield, *Ecclesial Cybernetics* (New York: Macmillan, 1973).

(4) John Calvin, *Institutes of the Christian Religion*, Book IV, chap. 1, par. 9.

(5) Emile Durkheim, *Elementary Forms of Religious Life* (London: Allen and Unwin, 1915), p. 47: "A religion is a unified system of beliefs and practices relative to sacred things, that is to say, things set apart and forbidden—beliefs and practices which unite into one single moral community called a Church, all those who adhere to them." It would seem inappropriate, to say the least, to claim that "the idea of religion is inseparable from that of the Church." Christian writers who would apply the word church to every religious community today would be insensitive to the possible imperialism and lack of flexibility in the word church.

(6) Douglas, op. cit., p. 64.

(7) Anthony Burgess, "For Permissiveness, with Misgivings," *New York Times Magazine,* July 1, 1973, p. 19.

(8) Alfred North Whitehead, *Science and the Modern World* (New York: Mentor, 1967), p. 88.

(9) See Maurice Friedman, *Touchstones of Reality* (New York: Dutton, 1972), p. 175.

(10) Ludwig Wittgenstein, *Philosophical Investigations* (Oxford: Blackwell, 1953), p. 47.

(11) Martin Buber, *The Knowledge of Man* (New York: Harper and Row, 1965), pp. 114ff.

(12) C. Wright Mills, *The Sociological Imagination* (New York: Oxford, 1959), p. 34.

(13) Harvey Cox, *The Seduction of the Spirit* (New York: Simon and Schuster, 1973).

(14) John A. T. Robinson, *The Difference in Being a Christian Today* (Philadelphia: Westminster, 1972).

(15) Ibid., p. 43.

(16) Theodore Roszak, *Where the Wasteland Ends* (Garden City: Doubleday, 1972).

(17) Ibid., pp. 446–65.

(18) Norman O. Brown, *Closing Time* (New York: Random House, 1973), p. 84.

(19) Ibid., p. 93.

(20) Paul Goodman, *New Reformation: Notes of a Neolithic Conservative* (New York: Vintage, 1970).

(21) Ibid., p. 191.

CHAPTER TWO

(1) See Michael Katz, *Class, Bureaucracy and Schools* (New York: Praeger, 1971), pp. 59ff.

(2) Michael Harrington, *Socialism* (New York: Saturday Review, 1972), p. 185.

(3) Robert Merton, *Social Theory and Social Structure* (Glencoe: Free Press, 1957), p. 200.

(4) Warren Bennis and Philip Slater, *The Temporary Society* (New York: Harper, 1968), pp. 53–76.

(5) See Max Weber, *Politics as a Vocation* (Philadelphia: Fortress, 1965).

(6) Quoted in Richard Sennett, *The Uses of Disorder* (New York: Knopf, 1970), p. 165.

(7) Robert Hunter, *The Storming of the Mind* (Garden City: Doubleday, 1972), p. 83.

(8) Quoted in Allen Graubard, *Free the Children* (New York: Pantheon, 1972), p. 4.

(9) See Robert Bellah, *Beyond Belief* (New York: Harper and Row, 1970).

(10) For the contrast of political cell and contemporary commune, see Hannah Arendt, *Crises of the Republic* (New York: Harcourt, Brace, Jovanovich, 1972), p. 232; and her earlier book, *On Revolution* (New York: Viking, 1965).

(11) See Juliet Mitchell, *Woman's Estate* (New York: Pantheon, 1971), p. 27.

(12) See Robert Michaelsen, *Piety in the Public School* (New York: Macmillan, 1970), p. 216.

(13) Maxine Greene, "And It Still is News," in *After Deschooling What?* ed. Alan Gartner, Colin Greer, Frank Reissman (New York: Perennial Library, 1973), pp. 134ff.

(14) Sennett, op. cit., p. 82.

(15) Everett Reimer, *School is Dead* (Garden City: Doubleday, 1971). The same applies to the parallel title of David Cooper, *The Death of the Family* (New York: Pantheon, 1970).

(16) Fred Newmann and Donald Oliver, "Education and Community," in *Religion in Public Education,* ed. Theodore Sizer (Boston: Harvard, 1967), pp. 184–227.

(17) Theodore Sizer, *Places for Learning, Places for Joy* (Boston: Harvard, 1973).

(18) Ibid., chapters 3 and 4.

(19) Statistics on women in the schools do not indicate progress in changing the system. In 1950, 6 percent of the high school principals were women; by 1973, 1.4 percent were women. In 1950, 50 percent of elementary school principals were women; by 1973, 19.6 percent were women. Yet 85 percent of the teachers in elementary schools are women. See *Where are the Women Superintendents?* (Arlington: National Council of Administrative Women in Education, 1973).

(20) Christopher Jencks, *Inequality* (New York: Basic Books, 1972).

(21) For example, Katz, op. cit., and Colin Greer, *The Great School Legend* (New York: Basic Books, 1972).

(22) Jencks, op. cit., p. 260.

(23) Robert Lynn and Elliot Wright, *The Big Little School* (New York: Harper and Row, 1971), p. 97.

CHAPTER THREE

(1) Quoted in Eric Voegelin, *Science, Politics and Gnosticism* (Chicago: Regnery, 1968), p. 64.

(2) Alfred North Whitehead, *Science and the Modern World* (New York: Mentor, 1967), p. 59.

(3) See Albert Camus, "Helen's Exile" in *The Myth of Sisyphus* (New York: Vintage, 1955), pp. 134–38.

(4) See Roger Garaudy, *From Anathema to Dialogue* (New York: Herder and Herder, 1966), p. 100.

(5) Harrington, *Socialism,* p. 345.

(6) Robert Jay Lifton, "The Struggle for Cultural Rebirth," *Harper's* (April, 1973), p. 86.

(7) Gordon Allport, *The Individual and his Religion* (New York: Macmillan, 1960).

(8) Gabriel Moran, *The Present Revelation* (New York: Herder and Herder, 1972).

(9) Heinz Zahrnt, *What Kind of God?* (Minneapolis: Augsburg, 1972), p. 169. Reprinted with permission.

(10) Wilfrid Desan, *The Planetary Man* (New York: Macmillan, 1973), p. 19.

(11) Louis Dupre, *The Other Dimension* (Garden City: Doubleday, 1972).

(12) Ibid., p. 320.

(13) Ibid., p. 322.

(14) One could go in the opposite direction and make belief the strongest, most comprehensive category so that knowledge is never more than a "case of belief." Although I think that this use of terms is less desirable than the one advocated here; the effect is similar; that is, belief would not be a word specifically appropriate for religion. For an interesting elaboration of this theme, see Joseph Pearce, *The Crack in the Cosmic Egg* (New York: Pocket Books, 1973).

(15) Robert Bellah, *Beyond Belief* (New York: Harper and Row, 1970), p. 220.

(16) Martin Buber, *Two Types of Faith* (New York: Harper, 1961), p. 34.

(17) Pierre Teilhard de Chardin, *Christianity and Evolution* (New York: Harcourt, Brace, Jovanovich, 1971), p. 99.

(18) Harvey Cox, *The Seduction of the Spirit* (New York: Simon and Schuster, 1973), p. 153.

(19) Juan Luis Segundo, *The Community Called Church* (New York: Orbis, 1973), p. 11.

(20) See William Leiss, *The Domination of Nature* (New York: Braziller, 1972), pp. 167–98.

(21) Gustavo Gutierrez, *A Theology of Liberation* (New York: Orbis, 1973).

(22) Ibid., pp. 301–2.

(23) Arthur Vogel, *Body Theology* (New York: Harper and Row, 1973).

(24) Examples of where experience is used, but in a restricted way, and the problem of faith remains: Bernard Lonergan, *Method in Theology* (New York: Herder and Herder, 1972); John Smith, *The Analogy of Experience* (New York: Harper and Row, 1973); Rosemary Haughton, *The Theology of Experience* (Paramus: Deus, 1972).

(25) R. D. Laing, *The Politics of Experience* (New York: Ballantine, 1967), p. 43.

(26) The scheme I use is parallel to the one Robert Bellah uses but he has a fivefold division: "Religion in the University: Changing Consciousness, Changing Structure," in *Religion in the Undergraduate Curriculum* (Washington: Association of American Colleges, 1972), pp. 14–15.

(27) Charles Reich, *The Greening of America* (New York: Random House, 1970).

(28) Ibid., pp. 16, 21, 288, 350.

(29) See Philip Nobile, ed., *The Con III Controversy* (New York: Pocket Books, 1971).

(30) See John Kenneth Galbraith, *Economics and the Public Purpose* (Boston: Houghton Mifflin, 1973), p. 231n. for a kind comment on Reich's book. *The Greening of America* was hardly more naive and unbalanced on the youth movement than a book at the same time by the renowned scholar Margaret Mead: *Culture and Commitment* (Garden City: Doubleday, 1970).

(31) Norman O. Brown, *Life Against Death* (New York: Vintage, 1959), pp. 273–74.

(32) Quoted in Hans Fortmann, *Discovery of the East* (Notre Dame: Fides, 1971), p. 21, n. 15.

(33) See John Mbiti, *African Religions and Philosophy* (Garden City: Anchor Books, 1970), pp. 19–36.

(34) Samuel Beckett, *Endgame* (New York: Grove, 1958), p. 49.

(35) E. E. Evans-Pritchard, *Nuer Religion* (London: Oxford, 1956), p. 2.

(36) Emile Durkheim, *Elementary Forms of Religious Life* (London: Allen and Unwin, 1915), p. 416.

(37) I. M. Lewis, *Ecstatic Religion* (Baltimore: Penguin, 1971), p. 205.

(38) As in Deane William Ferm, "Taking God Seriously," *Christian Century* (May 23, 1973), p. 598. The easy assumption of that masculine pronoun is central to the content and method of a Christian theology. See Mary Daly, *Beyond God the Father* (Boston: Beacon, 1973).

(39) See R. C. Zaehner, *Mysticism Sacred and Profane* (London: Oxford, 1961), pp. 170–71.

CHAPTER FOUR

(1) Robert Nisbet, *The Sociological Tradition* (New York: Basic Books, 1966), p. 18.

(2) See Clifford Geertz, "The Impact of the Concept of Culture on the Concept of Man," in *New Views of the Nature of Man*, ed. John Platt (Chicago: University of Chicago, 1965), pp. 93–118.

(3) See Arthur Osborne, *Buddhism and Christianity in the Light of Hinduism* (London: Rider, 1959); Alan Watts, *The Art of Contemplation* (New York: Pantheon, 1972).

(4) Ferdinand Toennies, *Community and Society* (New York: Harper, 1963).

(5) Kathleen Kinkade, *A Walden Two Experiment: The First Five Years of Twin Oaks Community* (New York: William Morrow, 1973).

(6) B. F. Skinner, *Beyond Freedom and Dignity* (New York: Knopf, p. 197).

(7) Kinkade, op. cit., pp. 44, 71–81, 191–99.

(8) Quoted in Hannah Arendt, *On Revolution* (New York: Viking, 1965), p. 252.

(9) Robert Townsend, "Petrie's Law," in *Intellectual Digest* (August, 1973), p. 56.

(10) See Nisbet, op. cit., p. 112.

(11) See Martin Buber, *Paths in Utopia* (Boston: Beacon, 1958).

(12) For uncritical celebration of temporariness, see Alvin Toffler, *Future Shock* (New York: Random House, 1970); a more restrained approval is found in Bennis and Slater, op. cit., pp. 77–96.

(13) See Harrington, *Socialism,* p. 304; a general description of the system's inequities in Galbraith, *Economics and the Public Purpose.*

(14) Robert Dahl, *After the Revolution* (New Haven: Yale, 1970), p. 114.

(15) See Elizabeth Janeway, "Breaking the Age Barrier," *Ms.* (April, 1973), pp. 5off.; Simone de Beauvoir, *The Coming of Age* (New York: Putnam, 1972).

(16) See Philip Slater, *The Pursuit of Loneliness* (Boston: Beacon, 1970), pp. 119–50.

(17) See Juliet Mitchell, *Woman's Estate* (New York: Pantheon, 1971), pp. 99–122; Germaine Greer, *The Female Eunuch* (New York: McGraw Hill, 1971), p. 8.

(18) Elizabeth Janeway, *Man's World, Woman's Place* (New York: William Morrow, 1971), p. 217.

(19) See Jerome Frank, *Sanity and Survival* (New York: Vintage, 1967).

(20) Walter Lippmann, *The Public Philosophy* (Boston: Little, Brown, 1955), p. 83.

(21) For the positive side of Jewish tradition on the feminine and God: Everett Gendler, "The Return of the Goddess," in *Ecology,* ed. Richard Sherrill (Richmond: John Knox, 1971), pp. 131–43; on the Virgin Mary in Christianity, see Mary Daly, *Beyond God the Father* (Boston: Beacon, 1973), pp. 81–92.

(22) See Nicolas Berdyaev, *Solitude and Society* (New York: Scribner, 1938), p. 65.

(23) See Thomas Berry, *Buddhism* (New York: Hawthorn, 1967), pp. 18–46.

(24) See ibid. pp. 100–105; Ninian Smart, *The Yogi and the Devotee* (London: Allen and Unwin, 1968).

(25) Albert Camus, *The Plague* (New York: Modern Library, 1948), p. 229.

(26) Lewis Mumford, *Myth of the Machine I: Technics and Human Development* (New York: Harcourt, Brace, Jovanovich, 1967), pp. 231–33.

(27) Hannah Arendt, *The Human Condition* (Chicago: University of Chicago, 1958), p. 55.

(28) Kathy Mulherin, "Memories of a (Latter-Day) Catholic Girl-

hood," in *New Theology No. 8,* ed. Martin Marty and Dean Peerman (New York: Macmillan, 1971), p. 82.

(29) See George Albert Coe, *A Social Theory of Religious Education* (New York: Scribner, 1917).

(30) See Loren Eiseley, *The Night Country* (New York: Scribner, 1971); Pierre Teilhard de Chardin, *The Future of Man* (New York: Harper and Row, 1964).

(31) Arthur C. Clarke, *Childhood's End* (New York: Ballantine, 1953).

(32) Rainer Maria Rilke, *Letters to a Young Poet* (New York: Norton, 1954), pp. 38–39.

CHAPTER FIVE

(1) Alfred North Whitehead, *The Aims of Education* (New York: Free Press, 1967), p. 14.

(2) Ivan Illich, *Deschooling Society* (New York: Harper and Row, 1971), p. 38.

(3) Quoted in Michaelsen, *Piety in the Public Schools,* p. 62.

(4) Quoted in ibid., p. 59.

(5) See Stephen Aarons, "Compulsory Education: The Plain People Resist," *Saturday Review* (Jan. 15, 1972), pp. 52–57.

(6) See Vine Deloria, *God is Red* (New York: Grosset and Dunlap, 1973), pp. 81, 260, 268.

(7) Gerald Jonas, *Visceral Learning* (New York: Viking, 1973).

(8) George Albert Coe, *What is Christian Education* (New York, Scribner, 1929), p. 238.

(9) Gabriel Moran, *Design for Religion* (New York: Herder and Herder, 1970), chapter one.

(10) The Catholic right-wing press now attacks the "new catechetics," which would seem to imply that they did accept an "old catechetics," but a few years ago it was "catechetics" they attacked. I have repeatedly requested that they not identify me as an advocate of the "new catechetics" since my views are not part of catechetics at all.

(11) Schoolboys of Barbiana, *Letter to a Teacher* (New York: Random House, 1970), p. 44.

(12) George Dennison, *The Lives of Children* (New York: Random House, 1969), p. 280. Reprinted with permission.

(13) Paulo Freire, *Pedagogy of the Oppressed* (New York: Herder and Herder, 1970), pp. 57–74.

(14) Sidney Jourard, *Disclosing Man to Himself* (Princeton: Van Nostrand, 1968), p. 195.

(15) Norman O. Brown, *Love's Body* (New York: Vintage, 1966), p. 245.

(16) W. R. Wees, *Nobody can Teach Anyone Anything* (Garden City: Doubleday, 1971).

(17) Paulo Freire, *Education for a Critical Consciousness* (New York: Seabury, 1973); Maria Montessori, *Education for a New World* (Madras: Kalakshetra, 1959).

(18) Sylvia Ashton-Warner, *Teacher* (New York: Simon and Schuster, 1963), p. 45.

(19) Carl Rogers notes that he uses more structure in a classroom than he did fifteen years ago. The teacher's structuring of material, requirement and environment can be a means of freedom. See *Freedom to Learn* (Columbus: Merrill, 1969), p. 73.

(20) See Christopher Lasch, "Inequality and Education," *New York Review of Books* (May 17, 1973), pp. 19–25.

(21) Louis Rubin, ed., *Facts and Feelings in the Classroom* (New York: Walker, 1973).

(22) Ibid., p. 108.

(23) Ibid., p. 16.

(24) See Herbert Read, *The Form of Things Unknown* (Cleveland: Meridian, 1967), pp. 15ff.

(25) See Richard Hofstadter, *Anti-Intellectualism in America* (New York: Vintage, 1963).

(26) Quoted in Evelyn Underhill, *Mysticism* (New York: Dutton, 1961), p. 333.

(27) Robert O'Neil and Michael Donovan, *Children, Church and God* (New York: Corpus, 1970).

(28) Ibid., p. 9.

(29) Ibid., p. 94.

(30) William James, *Talks to Teachers* (New York: Norton, 1958), p. 58.

(31) See Sidney Simon, et. al., *Values Clarification* (New York: Hart, 1972).

(32) F. R. Leavis, *D. H. Lawrence: Novelist* (New York: Clarion, 1969), p. 88.

(33) Claude Welch, *Religion in the Undergraduate Curriculum* (Washington: Association of American Colleges, 1972).

(34) The phrase was Justice Arthur Goldberg's in the case of Abington School District vs. Schempp.

(35) See Ninian Smart, *Secular Education and the Logic of Religion* (New York: Humanities, 1968), p. 90.

(36) Michaelsen, op. cit., p. 215.

(37) See Andrew Weil, *The Natural Mind* (Boston: Houghton Mifflin, 1972); Carlos Castaneda, *The Teachings of Don Juan* (New York: Ballantine, 1968).

(38) Aldous Huxley, *The Doors of Perception* (New York: Perennial Library, 1970), p. 69.

(39) See Freire, *Pedagogy of the Oppressed*, p. 53.

(40) Dennison, op. cit., p. 257f.

(41) See Robert Neale, *The Art of Dying* (New York: Harper and Row, 1973).

(42) Whitehead, *Aims of Education*, p. 39.

CHAPTER SIX

(1) John Taylor, *The Go Between God* (Philadelphia: Fortress, 1973), p. 147.

(2) Heinz Zahrnt, *What Kind of God?* (Minneapolis: Augsburg, 1972), p. 217.

(3) See Patrick Granfield, *Ecclesial Cybernetics* (New York: Macmillan, 1973), pp. 186, 209; for a bad attempt at proposing church reform on the narrowest authoritarian basis, see Louis Evely, *If the Church Is to Survive,* (Garden City: Doubleday, 1972).

(4) Jomo Kenyatta, *Facing Mount Kenya* (London: Martin Secker and Warburg, 1938), p. 186.

(5) For a parallel in the Hasidic movement see Maurice Friedman, *Touchstones of Reality* (New York: Dutton, 1972), p. 144; Elie Wiesel, *Souls on Fire* (New York: Random House, 1972), p. 142.

(6) See Werner Jaeger, *Paidea: The Idea of Greek Culture* (New York: Oxford, 1939).

(7) Warren Bennis and Philip Slater, *The Temporary Society* (New York: Harper, 1968), pp. 1–19.

(8) See Hannah Arendt, *On Violence* (New York: Harcourt, Brace and World, 1970).

(9) Pope Paul VI, "Address to Clergy and Religious of Rome," in *The Pope Speaks* (February, 1968), p. 38.

(10) Galbraith, *Economics and the Public Purpose*, p. 5.

(11) See Alexis de Tocqueville, *Democracy in America* (New York: Knopf, 1945), vol. 1, pp. 300–302.

(12) Harrington, *Socialism,* p. 325.

(13) Nisbet, *Sociological Tradition,* p. 284.

(14) Norman O. Brown, *Closing Time* (New York: Random House, 1973), p. 30.

(15) Malachi Martin, *Three Popes and a Cardinal* (New York: Farrar, Straus and Giroux, 1972).

(16) Essay printed in *New York Times,* July 13, 1973, op. ed. page.

(17) For the symbol of center in pottery, poetry and other things, M. C. Richards, *Centering* (Middletown: Wesleyan, 1964); John Fire/Lame Deer, *Lame Deer Seeker of Visions* (New York: Simon and Schuster, 1972), pp. 108–118.

(18) Samuel Beckett, *Molloy, Malone Dies, and The Unnameable, Three Novels* (New York: Grove, 1959), p. 406; Frederick Hoffman, *Samuel Beckett, The Language of Self* (New York: Dutton, 1964), pp. 133ff.

(19) See Mircea Eliade, *The Sacred and the Profane* (New York: Harper, 1959); and his "Ropes and Puppets," *The Two and the One* (New York: Harper, 1965), pp. 160–88.

(20) Robert Dahl, *After the Revolution* (New Haven: Yale, 1970), p. 83.

(21) See James McGregor Burns, *Uncommon Sense* (New York: Harper and Row, 1972), p. 169.

(22) Michael Rossmann, "Technology and Social Reconstruction," in *Ecology,* p. 113.

(23) See William McCready and Nancy McCready, "Socialization and the Persistence of Religion," in *The Persistence of Religion,* ed. Andrew Greeley and Gregory Baum (New York: Herder and Herder, 1973), p. 65ff.

(24) Gabriel Moran, "Religious Community: A Call to Be Born," in *National Catholic Reporter* (Dec. 18, 1970), p. 9.

(25) See Emily C. Hewitt and Suzanne Hiatt, *Women Priests: Yes or No?* (New York: Seabury, 1973), p. 19. I can agree with their comparing the feminist movement to the refusal of blacks to accept a separate-but-equal status. However, the significance of a black power movement as a parallel should not be overlooked, too.

(26) See Joseph Blenkinsopp, *Celibacy, Ministry, Church* (New York: Herder and Herder, 1968).

(27) See the discussion of the 1972 synod of bishops: *Ministerial Priesthood* and *Justice in the World* (Washington: USCC, 1972).

(28) Unfortunately, the term "women religious" is an exact parallel. One might get the impression that the right topic is being discussed because religious and women are the right words. But by reversing the normal order of the two words, we get a new abstraction which will probably be incapable of stabilizing the lives of women who have been nuns but is capable of blocking any coalition with the millions of religious women in the world.

(29) See Henri Nouwen, *Creative Ministry* (Garden City: Doubleday, 1971), pp. 2–20.

(30) See Herbert Richardson, *Nun, Witch, Playmate* (New York: Harper and Row, 1971).

(31) See William Johnston, *Chritsian Zen* (New York: Harper and Row, 1971), p. 92.

(32) In *The New Community* (New York: Herder and Herder, 1970), chapter 5, I presented a detailed plan of government for a religious group. After working with such a government for some years I would stand by all of the main parts of it though it could probably be simplified.

(33) My problem with the word leader is caught in a statement of Eugene Debs quoted by Michael Harrington, *The Accidental Century* (Baltimore: Penguin, 1965), p. 116: "I don't want you to follow me or anyone else. If you are looking for a Moses to lead you out of this capitalist wilderness, you will stay right where you are. I would not lead you into the promised land if I could, because if I could lead you in, someone else could lead you out."

(34) Analects, 5:25.

(35) Sidney Jourard, *Disclosing Man to Himself* (Princeton: Van Nostrand, 1968), p. 201; see also R. D. Laing, *The Politics of Experience* (New York: Ballantine, 1967), p. 128.

Index